Come Dance with Me

HÜMÜH Buddhist Stories

Higher Consciousness Publishing
2006

Come Dance with Me

ISBN-10: 0-932927-24-6
ISBN-13: 978-0-932927-24-8

HÜMÜH™
TRANSCENDENTAL AWARENESS INSTITUTE
The Jeweled Path of Transcendental Wisdom™

P.O. Box 2700, Oroville, WA 98844 USA
or P.O. Box 701, Osoyoos, B.C. V0H 1V0 Canada
Phone/fax (250) 446-2022 / Phone Orders (800) 336-6015
E-mail: office@HUMUH.org   Web Site: http://www.HUMUH.org

Table of Contents

Acknowlegement

Nothing is ever accomplished alone; it takes companion energy, and *Come Dance with Me* is no exception. Many people generously gave of themselves in order for this book to come into being.

First and foremost, thank you to Wisdom Master Maticintin, without whom, none of these stories would exist. It is an immeasurable gift to have a living Wisdom Master, who compassionately and patiently guides you to realize your true nature.

Thank you, especially, to all those who willingly opened themselves and shared their stories, being of service to the whole. Special thanks as well to the artists, proofreaders, and all the others who were involved in bringing this book into print. *Come Dance with Me* would not have happened without all of your wholehearted participation. May you have as much joy reading it as you did making it.

To all those
endeavoring
to live
the spiritual path.

Wisdom Master Maticintin

Wisdom Master Maticintin is a vessel of the Mind Treasure Teachings, gifted her by the Transhistorical Consciousness, meaning she attained enlightenment in another lifetime. The Wisdom Master is also the Founder and Spiritual Leader of HÜMÜH Buddhism: Transcendental Awareness, Path to Enlightenment. Currently in residence at the HÜMÜH Monastery in British Columbia, Wisdom Master Maticintin teaches there at Skycliffe Retreat Centre's Transcendental Awareness Institute. She also travels and teaches in the United States, Canada, and, occasionally, abroad.

Wisdom Master Maticintin is a noted author with many books to her credit, among them *Shaman of Tibet*, the story of Milarepa, and *The Golden Spiral: Handbook for Enlightenment*. She has been a student of Buddhism for more than 30 years and holds a Doctorate in Divinity, and is also the Shaman known as Winged Wolf.

While keeping up with an eleven-month Teaching schedule, the Wisdom Master maintains periods of solitude in between working with her students and takes time to be in companion energy with a herd of 50 wild deer, a horse named Spirit, a donkey called Pepe, and two rather royal cats addressed as Ichinen and Peaches.

She brought forth HÜMÜH in 1992 as an expression of primordial wisdom that directly addresses the Western body/mind connection. One of the manifestations of her dedication as a Teacher is the Home-Study program she has developed that enables students to work with her at a distance, as well as through on-site retreats and classes. The spiritual path of HÜMÜH began in the United States and has rapidly expanded into Canada, while developing membership in a variety of other countries.

Introduction

*C*ome *Dance with Me* is a collection of stories about students'
interactions with the Wisdom Master and the illuminations that
are born from these moments. A Wisdom Master is one who sees the
distinctions and subtleties of life, and as a result, displays clarity, a
clarity that sees beyond duality, through illusion, to the reality of the
oneness of all life. HÜMÜH has such a Teacher in Wisdom Master
Maticintin. HÜMÜH Buddhism is not secular; it is not a religion. It
is a way of life, a path of awareness. It is Buddhism in the truest sense
of the word: *awakening*—awakening to the divinity inherent in each
of us, realizing the oneness.

Some stories are brief exchanges in passing, and others took
weeks or years to unfold, but all have one thing in common—they
made the student aware of their habitual, self-serving behavior and
the life-situational obstructions it caused. This is a collection of stories about people learning to dance to the cadence of their divinity.

"Come dance with me," the Wisdom Master beckons, and a brave
few answer the call. At first, they are deaf to the music of divinity; the
din of their self-centered 'mind chatter' obscuring all other sound. But
with the Wisdom Master's guidance and encouragement, they begin
to quiet their minds, and in those first, brief pockets of silence, they
catch a few fleeting notes. This music stays with them, haunting, so
that they hunger for more. And as the music continues to resonate
inside them, they try to move in concert with it.

Their steps are awkward and stiff, like cardboard people, being
accustomed to the rigid dictates of their boxed mentalities. Sometimes,
when they focus on themselves, losing the music of the silence, they
trip over their own feet or remain locked in the same step. The

Wisdom Master sees all of this, and compassionately holds up a mirror for them to see their unnatural dance.

Through this, they become more aware of their aberrant steps, and as a result, persevere to maintain the quiet so that a natural movement can arise. Eventually, the silence begins to expand in them, so that the notes of divinity swell into melodies and movements. The Wisdom Master continues to teach them to dance through her own effortlessly smooth and joyous movement and through encouraging them to stretch themselves, pointing out a weighted arm here and a dragged foot there, showing them how to leap higher, how to float through the air.

Learning to dance is not always comfortable, but if they give themselves to the Wisdom Master's guidance, it is always enlightening, always uplifting, and a lightness of movement results. The student is brought to a place of selflessness where they can act for the good of the whole. No longer weighed down by the fabrications of a selfish ego and the confusion it creates, the student can leap and turn with clarity and effortlessness to the natural beat of the pure creative force, realizing that is who they are. Then, their dance becomes an outward expression of the primordial pulse, and they move in concert with the Wisdom Master, beckoning others to join the dance.

These stories are intended to be a source of upliftment to you, the reader. This is a book that you can read straight through or pick up and read a story at random. They are good 'anytime' stories. May they provide you with inspiration and clarity as you move along the spiritual path.

15

"In our sophisticated world that we live in, people have developed this sense that, if they read about something, they know about it,...or if they listen to some CD's about something, that they know about it; and yet, you know, you can listen to CD's of a great musican, and yet when you hear live music, it changes the whole thing. It is the same thing for spirituality. You can read books, and you can listen to CD's, and you can talk to people, but when you actually come in close contact with a spiritual Master, you have a whole different sense of spirituality that you couldn't acquire any other way....This business of coming in contact with the *source* is what's really important in life. It's what you actually experience in the presence of one who lives spiritual Teachings that makes the difference....There is a richness of flavor, of love and continuity that can't be experienced from a CD, an experience of energy that may be indicated in a CD or a book, but its actual vitality isn't the same as being present to it....How very important it is to actually have spiritual experience, not just hear about it; anybody can hear about things, but it is quite different to participate in it. Participating in it means that you are in that presence, and you open yourself to that and experience that vitality as a nurturing component that enters yourself; and while you are in that presence, you can feel that aliveness within yourself....You have to give of yourself at some point in order to have an experience of any kind, but if you truly want the epxiereince, it is there to have. And that is the way all life should be lived, experientially."

Wisdom Master Maticintin

The Dance

❝ Y*ou have to let go,"* the Wisdom Master told me quietly as we left the Temple after the evening sitting.

I was glued to my difficulty with fear. I wanted to let go, but my version of 'letting go' was resistance, not release, and I was 'frozen,' stuck.

"This is just not working," I said to the Wisdom Master as I blindly headed off to my room at the loghouse. I felt empty and alone. In my room I dressed for bed, hoping to escape everything in sleep.

Then, there was a knock at the door. I opened it and was surprised to see the Wisdom Master and another apprentice standing there as if it was the most natural thing in the world to be there. The Wisdom Master looked at me and asked what I was wearing. I looked down at my 'shorty' summer p.j.'s.

"They are pajamas," I replied, as the unreal, dreamlike scene unfolded. I had wanted to be alone, but at the same time, I was relieved that she was there.

"Put on some shoes and come outside," the Wisdom Master instructed.

I did so, wondering what would come next and walked out of my room into the glowing, warm, summer evening.

"I want you to do Tai Kar Chi for twenty minutes before bed every night," the Wisdom Master told me. I agreed, but did not have the foggiest idea what Tai Kar Chi was. The Wisdom Master briefly showed me some movements. As I watched her graceful, effortless "dance," suddenly nothing else existed. All thoughts about my difficulty were gone. All I saw was the Wisdom Master, and my nightmare seemed to have turned into a beautiful dream.

When the Wisdom Master and the apprentice left, I began to do my own dance. I was clumsy at first, but when I relaxed, I let my arms swing freely as I 'became' the trees in the orchard and the clouds in the sky. Very quickly, however, I noticed that I was not dancing alone. There was what seemed like millions of hungry mosquitoes that were joining me with a feast in mind. *'Well, then,'* I thought, *'we will all just dance together.'* But first, I went back into my room and covered my skimpy pajamas with long pants and a long-sleeved shirt. I was ready. For at least twenty minutes, I twirled, and floated, and bowed, and 'flew.' I did not care how I looked. All I 'saw' was the Wisdom Master. I had begun to dance to a 'different tune.'

Look for the Dance

It was August and 'monsoon season' in Arizona. Wisdom Master Maticintin took me into a yard surrounded by trees, and we sat in their midst.

She said, *"Watch, and tell me what you see."*

I looked around....the sky was dark and threatened rain; lightning creased high clouds in the distance. The wind was blowing hard, and the gusts carried bits of earth. The tree branches waved back and forth, leaves moving one way, then another...I related those observations to the Wisdom Master.

She smiled at me, and then said, *"The trees wear clothes so that you can see the wind dance with them."*

That comment changed the way I see our planet, and I now look for the 'dance' and smile with gratitude.

Each Raindrop Is an Apprentice

The Wisdom Master was sitting in the Temple before another
apprentice and I arrived. After a short *'Hello,'* she asked that I
sing my words to her. I thought to myself, *'This is different.'* I sang a
'good morning' to her as we exchanged smiles. She greeted the other
apprentice upon his arrival, and we prepared to HÜM. There was
complete silence; the only sound heard was that of our breath as we
inhaled and exhaled deeply.

There were no other sounds but the HÜM....no birds chirping,
no raindrops falling on the roof, no sounds of dogs walking on the
cobbled rock path. There was nothing but the sound of the three of us
HÜMing.

The HÜMing became like a union. It started with a deaf apprentice HÜMing close to the same pitch that Wisdom Master Maticintin
and I were HÜMing. The union of Song continued out of the Temple to
the environment around us. Birds began chirping to the HÜM, ducks
started to quack to the HÜM, frogs croaked, the geese sang, and soft
raindrops added to the sound of the HÜM. And yes, even structural
creaking sounds from the frame of the Temple enmeshed with the
song. It was like an orchestrated, harmonious sound.

At the time, I did not think about such questions as, *'How could
this be? How could someone who is deaf pick up when the Wisdom
Master shifted pitches? How could there be so many different sounds?'*

We all stopped HÜMing about the same time, with a few birds
adding an extra dangling chirp or two at the end. Then there was
silence, long silence, followed by the Wisdom Master's, *"May the Blessings Be."* I looked at the Wisdom Master and saw a luminescence
around her as well as around the other apprentice.

That morning, the Wisdom Master asked us to join her for a short walk. We followed her to a hill above the river and just looked out. My, oh my! What a sight to behold. There were soft raindrops falling in the river, negative ions were abundantly in the air, and the sound of a distant bird could be heard from afar. I was mesmerized by the softness of the raindrops falling on the river. The Wisdom Master read my mind and said, *"Each raindrop is an apprentice."*

As she spoke, the raindrops started to multiply. We stood there for some time, and then left. That day was a magical day. There was magic everywhere.

Being Spontaneous

The year that the Stupa was finished, I had the opportunity to work with the Wisdom Master in the Stupa garden. For the garden beds around the perimeter, the dirt had been dug out and replaced with top soil. The dirt that had been removed was in mounds. Instead of moving the dirt again, the Wisdom Master decided that these piles would become gardens. She was arranging stones in small circles or ovals, and it was my job to plant flowers. We had an assortment of annuals to choose from.

Being in her presence, I did not have to think of what to do. There was no premeditation. After several hours, I climbed down from the mound and was standing there thinking. Wisdom Master Maticintin said to me, *"What are you doing?"* I said, *"I am trying to figure out what to do for the next little area."* I was trying to plan. She then said to me that I should quit for the day because I was tired.

Up until that experience, I had not really understood how you could act spontaneously in some projects. I was used to having a blueprint, a pattern for things. When I had begun, I had been in her energy and it just happened, but then I got tired and reverted to habitual patterns.

Outmoded Habitual Behaviors

On my knees in the Temple, I was offered the Lay Monk Vow by the Wisdom Master. After taking my vow, Wisdom Master Maticintin handed me the registry to sign my name. I scrawled out my name in a habitual, rapid way that came out as a squiggly line, as if it were just some check I'd written at the grocery store.

The Wisdom Master paused and looked directly at me. She said, *"When you sign a vow, you are making a promise. To sign quickly and illegibly is to present an energy that is hurried and uncaring."*

She went on to say, *"When you take that vow, you are promising to honor and protect your Wisdom Master, the Teachings and the spiritual community. Your signature denotes that you do not appear to care about the vow or your spiritual family. It is so unintelligible that it looks like you are trying to hide something."*

Then she asked me, *"Did you really want to take the Vow?"*

"Oh, yes, I did," I replied earnestly. Her words sank in deeply and cut right to the place where my habitual, outmoded behaviors had blocked my awareness and delayed my ability to grow in compassion.

Since that day, I have been sensitive to my signature, looking at it as an extension of my own energy and aware that what I put out in thought, word and deed generates karma. I really desire to emanate energy that is for the good of the whole. This lesson has helped me on many levels to become more aware of that.

The Impact of Emotions

One day, I was driving along in a city on a four-lane road. The day was pleasant, and my morning had been easy and productive. Suddenly, I was consumed with waves of intense anger. Fortunately, I was conscious enough to see the anger arising and realize that it was not mine, but I had no idea where it had come from. I was saying to myself, *'What in the world is happening here; there is no reason for the anger."* Within moments of the anger's arising, the traffic, which had been fairly heavy but smooth, began going nuts. People started switching lanes, cutting each other off, and blowing horns. As I watched in amazement, I realized that I had to get off the road before something happened. I managed to work my way over to the shoulder and pulled off and parked. Getting out of the car, I walked into the grass and sat down for a bit, waiting for my emotions to settle down. The traffic seemed back to normal by now. After calling in my mind on the Wisdom Master for help, I felt my body quieting and my feelings subsiding.

I returned to the car and proceeded about my day with no further problems. Upon returning to Skycliffe, I told the Wisdom Master about my experience, and she told me that the anger was a releasing of some old karma, and it did not matter if I was aware of the story behind the anger. Then she told me that the reaction of the traffic was the other drivers feeling the burst of anger from me. I was stunned by the realization that emotions could produce such a dramatic effect on others, who were seemingly unrelated to my process. Now, I am ever-watchful for the clues and feedback about how my energy is affecting my environment. I try to be more aware of how my emotions impact those around me.

Companion Energy

In the spring, we were getting the Mandala Garden around the Stupa ready for planting. We planted dahlias a little too early, and a frost hit them quite hard. We cut them back and hoped they would recover. As we were planting lobelias and alyssum later, I remembered Wisdom Master Maticintin's telling us to plant the young, vibrant plants in amongst the ailing ones because their vital energy would help the others to become vital as well. It wasn't long before the weakened dahlias began showing buds, and they bloomed all summer. I could see that the strength of one vital plant indeed assisted another through its energy, and was reminded that this is so with other living beings, as well.

Anger Is Anger

One Sunday morning, I drove into the grounds to unload some things that I purchased the day before. I had been to town and had some heavy things that I needed to take to my house. I had a fleeting perception that maybe my timing was not right, but my little-self overruled my intuition, and I quietly drove in, unloaded, and drove out again.

The Wisdom Master called me in later and told me that I had disturbed the silence of the Sunday morning during a time when everything was to be quiet. I apologized and inwardly chastised myself for not listening to my gut feeling. As I was leaving, the Wisdom Master said that I was angry. I immediately replied that I was not angry at *her,* and she said, *"What's the difference?"*

I realized that anger is anger, no matter where it is placed, since we are all one.

Circles

It was my first visit to *'Between the Wind,'* the Wisdom Master's former residence on Orcas Island, Washington. That morning, the Wisdom Master had come to me and said, *"Each of the remaining days that you are here, I would like you to find time to walk 200 laps around the Happy House in Third Eye Vision. You can start now."*

'Wow!' I thought. *'I wonder how long that will take?'* So off I went to the little meditation house and began circling it. I was on lap #5 when an apprentice came down from the Wisdom Master's office and said, *"Please, start over. You are walking counter-clockwise, and you need to move in a clockwise direction."* Stuffing my hands in my jacket pockets, I began again. I was on lap #10 when the apprentice came down and said, *"The Wisdom Master would like you to take your hands out of your pockets, and let your arms move freely at your sides as you walk in Third Eye Vision. Please, begin again."*

Around and around I went. Quickly, I noticed that my mind was chattering to itself, *'Well, I hope I'm doing it right now. It's going to take a long time to do 200 laps if I have to keep starting over, etc., etc.'* As I heard these useless thoughts, I began to chuckle. This surely could not be Third Eye Vision. What did it matter how long it took? I was 'on the Wisdom Master's clock,' which was timeless. I had come here to be with her, to learn from her, to do whatever she asked. If she wanted me to walk around the meditation hut, that was what I would do, how I would learn. It was kind of a privilege to be allowed to circle the meditation house with the trail of my energy. I needed to keep that energy as clean, and loving, and conscious as I could while I did that.

I began to enjoy the exercise, both physically and spiritually.

My awareness heightened. Each lap was a little different—the light changed; I saw a flower I hadn't noticed before. I felt my senses extending to include larger and larger awareness of the environment. As the days went by, when I made my circles, I felt very connected to the Wisdom Master, even though she was nowhere in sight. A rhythm developed in my movement, and I felt in harmony with the circling of the planets. I began to see the little, shining particles in the air before me.

I had also become very aware of the small insects and worms that traveled the ground I walked upon. They had never appealed much to me before; often, I had found them nuisances, but now I felt very close to them. I was sorry I had ever killed an ant or a spider. We were fellow travelers. I realized that these 'small kin' also 'belonged to the Wisdom Master,' were her 'students,' making their evolutionary circles of discovery on this property, where they were safe to be themselves and follow their destiny.

Road Story

The Wisdom Master had often reminded us that she is with us even when we are traveling. I always thought of that on my days off and found the quiet time alone in the car to be a time when it was easy to be aware of the divine presence. She had also warned us often not to daydream while driving but to be fully, consciously present so that no sentient life would be harmed by our lack of attention. The winter roads sometimes made this kind of mindfulness especially critical.

I was returning from a northern town one January evening, happy, as always, to be nearing Skycliffe. The roads were snowy with patches of black ice here and there, but I had done fine and was now on Kettle Valley Road nearing the 11km marker. It was a beautiful night, the moon was almost full, and the snow reflected that light. The moon hung white and luminous over the valley, and I thought how like the Wisdom Master it was, shedding its radiance on all the sentient creatures.

I was driving slowly and mindfully and slowed even further as the road made a tilted curve, banking to the left through some granite outcroppings. Suddenly, the whole car began to go into a slow, lateral "slide" toward the ditch and the bank of granite on the left. I knew I couldn't hit the brakes so I tried to turn the wheel to the left in the direction of the skid. That only pointed the nose of the car directly down toward the ditch and head-on into the rocks.

Everything went into slow motion then, and with all my heart, I cried outloud, *"No! No! No!...Maticintin, Master, Master!"* As I did so, the car lifted free of the road, turned in mid-air, and the rear wheels of the car sank into the snowy ditch, just missing the granite

31

outcroppings. As the car settled, the front wheels managed to stay hooked up onto the shoulder of the road, and I found myself at a forty-five degree angle, staring up out of the windshield at the radiant face of the full moon! Nothing crashed, nothing exploded. There was no smell of leaking gas or oil. The engine was still running. I was unhurt. The lights shone on the very tops of the pine trees across the road. I turned off the ignition, and there was a pristine, total, all-embracing silence.

The back seat of the car was up to the windows in snow. Flowers for the Wisdom Master's office were strewn across the seat, but unharmed. With effort, I forced the driver's door open and clambered out into hip-deep snow. I scribbled my name and the monastery phone number on a scrap of paper, stuck it under the windshield wiper, and hauled myself up onto the road. It was dark both directions, and I couldn't remember which way the nearest house with a phone might be. I knew I was still about 14 km from Skycliffe. There wasn't a car in sight; all was moonlight and silence.

Gratefully, I opened my heart/mind to the Wisdom Master, hoping she would sense I was all right and thanking her. And all at once, I knew which direction to walk. Of course, help would come from the direction of the Wisdom Master! I set out on the moonlit road walking toward Skycliffe, and it felt like I was walking in the Wisdom Master's heart.

About a half-mile later, I saw a truck coming from the direction of the monastery. A man and his wife pulled up and gave me a ride back to the phone by the Westbridge store so I could let folks at Skycliffe know where I was. Then the couple took me to where a fellow apprentice was living, and she kindly drove me back to Skycliffe. During that whole time, no other car ever came by, from either direction.

As it turned out, there was absolutely no damage to my car. All it needed was a hefty tug from a tow truck the next morning.

But more importantly, I was vividly and gratefully aware of how present the Divine Love and Protection of the Wisdom Master is if we are mindful, if we call out to It in times of need, times when we realize that all we truly want is to have the opportunity to go on learning how to live from that same divinity that is awakening within us.

How blessed we are to have such a Living Wisdom Master in our lives!

Asking for Help

I had been having some physical challenges and was going through a bad time. Wisdom Master Maticintin was aware of this, but I was trying to 'do it on my own' because of feelings of pride. I didnt want to admit that I didn't have a handle on my problems, and that I was allowing bad health to affect me. I was frustrated and suffering. One day she phoned me, and this is what I remember her saying, *"You know, I cannot help you unless you ask for help."* Such a basic thing, and I knew it, but because of my pride, I had put it out of my mind. After she hung up, I immediately sat down on my meditation cushion and cried out for help; and, yes, I did receive the help that I needed.

Encouragement

66 *E* *veryone has S O M E T H I N G,"* the Wisdom Master softly said to me as I sat in her office on the meditation cushion in front of her. We had been talking about a health issue of mine. She had been working with me for some time, nourishing me with the Teachings and with love, and I was learning to be mindful, to follow my heart and trust. I felt that much healing had taken place on the 'inside,' but that day, I opened my heart to the Wisdom Master, saying that I was feeling a little discouraged by not yet having seen 'progress' on the 'outside,' on a physical level.

I remember feeling the Wisdom Master's love wrap around me as she said that what I was doing could be of help to others.

"Yes," I said as I breathed in what seemed like fresh air. I felt a warmth in my heart, and I remember noticing that the room had somehow become brighter. I stopped staring at myself as the thought of helping others, of doing all I could for the good of the whole, filled me with joy.

Pride

The Wisdom Master had been taking another apprentice and me with her to learn how to put the coat on Spirit, the Wisdom Master's horse. Lately, Spirit had not been cooperating with the stable hands, so the Wisdom Master was re-training me and also training someone new. As the Wisdom Master walked with us on the way to the barn, she had to remind us to quiet our minds. I had been re-minded many times how essential it was to have a quiet mind while working with the horses. Again, on the way back from the barn, she had to remind us to quiet our minds. Finally, she told us to lay down with our faces to the ground.

The Wisdom Master later talked to me about my being a prideful person. As I reflected on this and saw the extreme the Wisdom Master had to go through to get my attention, I decided to look at my attitude during the training sessions. I saw that I was nervous while being trained by the Wisdom Master and was always focused on myself, chattering in my mind- *'What should I be doing? Should I ask questions? I hope she doesn't ask me to put the coat on while she and the other apprentice watch,'* and on and on. Because I was always focused on myself, I was never really present to just observing, with a quiet mind, so I could learn. I saw my lack of wholeheartedness to learn. I was really just biding my time until the training would be over, and no one would be watching, then I would find my own way of getting the coat on, ignoring the danger my pride would be placing me in with a 1,500-pound animal with whom I had already had problems.

Quiet

In a conversation with Wisdom Master Maticintin, she shared how humans have made many technological advances, and wouldn't it be nice to have a truly soundproof car, so a person could ride quietly with no outer distractions. *"Yes, that would be nice,"* I responded. She looked at me and asked, *"Then why don't you have a quiet mind?"* I'd been zapped with something to look at.

Give an Inch and Take a Mile

Six apprentices took an afternoon walk with Wisdom Master Maticintin. The walk began with the Wisdom Master's walking arm-in-arm with two of the apprentices. There was soft laughter and an exchange of many smiles. However, the walk ended on a different note. Let me explain....

In the course of the walk, the voices of those walking with her started to get a little louder, and the energy started to become scattered. The Wisdom Master continued to walk but did not talk. We apprentices continued to talk. It goes without saying that if we had been in companion energy with the Wisdom Master, we would have effortlessly fallen into silence with her. We did not.

At one point, the Wisdom Master stopped, turned to us, and said, *"Please, quiet your mouths and your minds."*

As she spoke, I thought to myself, *'What are we really doing here? This is no summer camp outfit.'* She initially had written, *"This is a training center, the environment should reflect that. Bear in mind, your visit is a time for you to take a leap in consciousness."*

Recalling that, I thought, *'Well, surely, we did not come here to look for distractions...we have enough of them at home. This is a place to spend time with the Wisdom Master. Of course, we just got carried away!'* The saying, *'give an inch, take a mile'* rang in my ears. I was a little embarrassed that the Wisdom Master had to tell us to be quiet. We should have known that since she had stressed the importance of silence for the previous two days.

38

Looking In

" M ost (humans) are operating from mind chatter, thinking about this, thinking about that; always mulling everything over. There can be no companion energy with one who is entrapped by the mind." This is a quote from one of the Wisdom Master's books.

I remember the first, one-week retreat I had at Skycliffe. I was nervous, unrelaxed, trying to appear as I thought the Wisdom Master wanted me to be. I was going to be flawless. It wasn't long before the Wisdom Master told me to stop looking at myself and gave me the practice of not looking in the mirror during my stay. I was excited by this task and surprised at the freedom it gave me.

But I had no idea that looking in a mirror was a metaphor for the all-pervasive habit I had of relating to the world through looking in at myself. It was years later during a teaching that the Wisdom Master asked me to '*look at her*' and '*stop looking in.*' My eyes went wide open, and my head cocked forward, straining with intensity to look at the Wisdom Master. She kept repeating *"Look at me."* With every repetition, my head and eyes leaned forward to meet her gaze. She finally said, *"You are still looking in at yourself."*

I was exasperated because I so wanted to look out of myself but couldn't grasp how to do it. After a time of reflection, I realized that as I was outwardly looking directly at the Wisdom Master, inwardly, I was looking at myself; I was looking at her while asking all kinds of questions inside my head: '*What does she want of me? What is she seeing as she looks at me? Is she upset with me? Does she like me? What am I doing wrong?*' etc. etc.

This story is a way of saying that the Wisdom Master has been patiently and consistently teaching me to look out of myself so that I can begin to align my point of view with hers, so that she can teach me in companion energy. Otherwise, I cannot move forward as I continue to see all life through my opinions, attitudes, fears and habits. I have grown accustomed to using others as a reflective mirror, but only in terms of how they see me. Old habits die hard. But as I have begun to look out of myself, I am finding the freedom and joy of being unencumbered by a critical, self-centered mind.

Facing Fear

I was visiting the Wisdom Master with several other students. The house was crowded, and the Wisdom Master said maybe someone would have to sleep outside. I was instantly wary. Not only did I not want to be uncomfortable and inconvenienced by sleeping outside in a tent with no bed and no bathroom, but I was afraid. I had never slept outside by myself. In fact, I had never slept outside. I was not even always comfortable sleeping inside. Occasionally, when I was really nervous, I slept with the light on. I could not possibly be the one to sleep outside in a tent away from everyone.

Although I tried to hide my discomfort, I knew that the Wisdom Master sensed it. Eventually, the Wisdom Master looked at me and asked me to go for a walk with her. We went out the back door and walked away from the house. We climbed over a slight rise and sat down. None of the lights were visible. It was very, very dark—without any of the city lights that I was used to. I could tell that the Wisdom Master was totally comfortable, and I felt safe with her. I told her that I was afraid of the night, of being alone in the dark. I was afraid of things that could not be seen. The Wisdom Master had me relax by sensing the 'feeling' of the evening. I heard the Wisdom Master say that the same things existed in the dark that existed in the light. That this did not change. Night and day were essentially the same, except that, at night, because of the quiet, senses were heightened. As I relaxed at the Wisdom Master's side, I could feel the gentleness of the night. It was soft, like velvet, and not of itself dangerous. The fear was in the mental images that I had. That night I slept in the tent, and it was my first step to learning to be at ease in the darkness.

Years later, I heard the Wisdom Master say, in an almost off-hand way, that fear was mostly vanity. That comment caught me off guard. How could fear be vanity? Then I flashed on that night I had not wanted to sleep outside in the tent. The fact was that my first thoughts had been about MY discomfort. I wanted a bed and proximity to the bathroom. Someone else with camping experience, I reasoned, should sleep outside. But what about the fears of things that really happen? And then I saw the mean truth. My real fear(s) were, first, that something would happen to ME: anything from something simple, and maybe just embarrassing, to something really terrible and painful. Second, my fear was that something would happen to MY family, MY friends, MY acquaintances, people I knew and cared about. If fearful things had to happen, then I wanted them to happen to faceless, nameless others to whom I was not connected. My fears were essentially about ME not being hurt. Vanity.

This realization shook me to my core. Unconditional love and compassion could not even begin to exist in me with such vanity.

Fruit of Thought

My dog was sick. I was telling the Wisdom Master about it in a phone call. I had picked the little Sheltie when she was only six-weeks-old. She had been the runt of the litter, but more feisty and alert than her larger, calmer sisters. I had been seated on the breeder's couch with my legs crossed at the ankles and extended in front of me as I watched the puppies move and play. While her litter mates ambled around the 'showing room,' this one had aimed straight for me, run up my legs and stood on my chest staring into my eyes and wagging her tail furiously, as though we shared a secret, as though we were old friends.

Now, though only three-years-old, my little buddy suddenly had a large growth blocking her small intestine. *"The vet says it's as large as a peach pit,"* I told the Wisdom Master, who quickly interrupted my worried recital. *"Oh,"* she said, *"maybe only the size of a plum pit."*

'What?' I thought. 'What kind of answer was that? What did she mean by it? That's what the vet said, and he was looking at the X-rays.' But I didn't say that. I didn't say anything. I let the pause in our conversation extend. By now, I had been an apprentice long enough to know that the Wisdom Master was <u>always</u> Teaching. Always!

Something started to dawn in me, but I didn't have words for it yet. I had been seeing that 'peach pit' in my mind, over and over, ever since the vet said it; but now, I could see a plum pit and it was definitely smaller. The image had changed and so had my emotional reaction to it. *"OK,"* I said slowly. *"Maybe only as big as a plum pit."* I was calm now. Open. Wondering.

"Yes," she said again. *"Maybe smaller. Maybe not so serious."*

43

"*OK,*" I said. "*Thank you. I'll remember that.*" When I hung up, I realized my whole attitude had lightened, shifted away from a fixed, negative conclusion. It was now open-ended, flexible. There were possibilities again now that the 'freeze-frame' of the negative image didn't fill my mind. Things change in the body all the time. This had come about suddenly. Maybe it could also go away. I wasn't grabbing on to the situation any longer. Just open to possibilities, to whatever would be the best.

A few days later, they x-rayed again. "*It's the darndest thing,*" the vet said, "*but the growth has shrunk. It's definitely smaller.*" A week later, he said, "*Well, I don't really know why or how, but the growth is gone. If it weren't for the scar on the lining of the intestine, I wouldn't know it had ever been there.*"

Releasing the Old

I had a dream in which I was very carefully taking apart a car, cleaning each part very thoroughly, and then putting it on a bench. I later asked the Wisdom Master about the dream, and she said it was reflective of my disassembling my old self. As she said those words, a shiver ran up my spine, and I felt an opening occur. As I began to look at my life and the impact of my apprenticeship, I could see suddenly how the old, unwanted ways were slowly dropping away. Sometimes, I would cling dearly, and sometimes, I would just let go. I also realized that there are those times as I disassemble my old, unwanted ways of life, I am left with the realization that what was, no longer works or exists, and yet, what is to be, has not yet arrived. It is in those times that I have to surrender to the flow of my life and trust the Wisdom Master will be there to guide me. I am most happy to say that the Wisdom Master is always present for me, and it is up to me to open myself in order to receive what is offered.

Grieving

A few years ago, someone I loved very much passed away. It was not the first time I had lost someone close to me, but I hadn't dealt very well with the previous loss. I had refused to let go, and I had created a great amount of suffering because of my attachment. I didn't want to do the same thing this time. I didn't want to get caught up in the same cycle. But now somone else who had been close to me had died. About a week after the funeral, I asked the Wisdom Master if she would help me.

She said, *"Loving someone never goes away, and so continuing to love someone who has translated is very natural. And when someone you love dies, a piece of your heart has been removed; it is truly painful. And the pain is real, which means that time is the only healer. It may take months or even a year, but until then, there is something you can do. Every time you recall your friend's face or think of them in any way, bless their memory in the name of the Divine Consciousness, then do some act of service in their name. In that way, you will make good karma for them and yourself as well, and that will uplift them, and your memory of them will uplift you. Be patient, and, if the tears flow of their own accord, bless the tears and then again do service in their name."*

A few days later, I was working in my apartment. I had come to a stopping place and was thinking about taking a break and running down to the corner store, but I hadn't made up my mind yet, and so I just sat there silently looking out my window. In that moment of pause, when one thing had finished and the next thing had yet to begin, an image of my deceased loved one flashed in my mind, and tears began to fill my eyes. I swallowed as a lump formed in my throat, the feeling of loss almost overwhelming. But then I remembered the Wisdom Master's words, and I blessed her memory in the name of the Divine Consciousness, smiling softly at the remembered joy of that moment. Then, I thought of the other part of what the Wisdom Master had said…to do service in my loved one's name. As that thought occurred to me, an image came to mind of a homeless man who usually hung out around the store where I had been thinking of going. I quickly got up, grabbed my bag, and headed out the door. As I got closer, I could see that the man was standing outside the door, asking people for change as they came out. I didn't have any money on me, so I got some cash from the ATM machine. When I came out of the store, he asked me in the manner of one expecting to be refused, if I had any change to spare. I smiled warmly at him and handed him the money that I had gotten from the ATM machine, silently saying I did it in my loved one's name. He glanced at the money in his hand, and his face lit up, and he thanked me. This great feeling of love and warmth filled me; all feelings of loss were gone. An image of my loved one's smiling face popped into my head, and I thought, *'What a fitting way to honor her memory, and what a wonderful way to give to her.'* It felt so uplifting to know that I could still give to her.

And so I continued to do that over the weeks that followed. The tears still came, but I blessed them and allowed them to flow. Sometimes, I stumbled and got caught up in the emotions, but then I would remember the Wisdom Master's words. Eventually, the tears began to taper off, and the memories that surfaced were no longer barbed with grief.

Almost a year later, I talked to the Wisdom Master again about how I dealt with this loss, looking at how I allowed certain mind sets to create obstacles for me.

She said, *"Your love for your friend was very special. As long as you remember her, she continues to live in you."*

When I heard those words, I smiled, feeling the truth in them. With this realization, a powerful energy surged through me, my heart swelled with love, filling me with confidence and strength.

The Gift

Late one evening, our son called us with news about his own infant son. The baby was having chronic difficulty breathing, and the doctor had said that it could be something that would be outgrown, or it could be more serious. They needed more tests to find out. Our son was in tears and told us that he could not shake the feeling that the baby would die. He also remarked that he and his wife were unable to communicate without anger towards each other, because of their fear that they might lose their son. I told him to take one step at a time, and that I would speak to the Wisdom Master. He said that he would be grateful.

The next morning, I spoke to the Wisdom Master, and as I sat at the foot of her desk, I looked into her somber but calm face as she spoke. I remember that she told me that unless our son and his wife could pull together in love, the child would be affected by their doubt and dissension. The baby would die, and as a result, the marriage would fail. She told me that this was a time for me to step in. I was to go directly home and speak to our son. She advised me not to think of what I would say, just to open my heart. I felt like I was in a vacuum as the enormity of what was happening engulfed me. As if in response, the Wisdom Master quietly said, *"I will be with you,"* and I felt her love as it entered my heart like a promise. I stood up with resolve, not really knowing anything, and knowing that I did not know anything, and I left her office. My husband and I headed for home immediately.

When I spoke to our son, I remember opening up my heart and sharing with him some of the difficult times we experienced with him when he was growing up. I said that we loved him and never gave up on him. I reminded him that he had never given up on himself. I asked him not to give up on his son. When I finished, our son thanked me with love in his voice, and we hung up.

Later, our son told me that he and his wife had put aside their fears the best they could and had begun to pull together. Their child's difficulty simultaneously lessened.

Constant Awareness

It was a hot day. Spiritual students were busy mixing concrete, which was then troweled into buckets and lifted by the tractor to workers shaping the Stupa dome. The emptied buckets were then dropped into the waiting hands of workers on the ground to be refilled. The work was exciting as each of us lovingly played a part in building the Stupa. Eager to be of continued help, I resisted taking a break. Looking at Wisdom Master Maticintin, she motioned for me to follow her. I was led to a grassy spot beneath an apple tree where we both lay down, and I was shown stretching exercises for my lower back. In the midst of all the construction details, the needs of the individual workers were always in her awareness.

Night Vision

It was three in the morning on a warm, August night during the very first empowerment with the Wisdom Master. Those attending were bedded down in bunkbed cabins scattered throughout a wooded camp in Oak Creek Canyon, near Sedona, Arizona. Suddenly, I was wide awake.

I could hear the breathing rhythms of my five cabin buddies. I could hear the ripple and riffle of Oak Creek flowing nearby. It had taken a long time for the camp to settle into sleep. I didn't want to disturb anyone, but I felt like I just had to get outside into the desert night for a little while. Slipping silently out of my bunk, I decided I wouldn't take a flashlight. I had good night vision. I tiptoed out and decided to climb the hill to the bathroom.

The night was beautiful. As I made my way slowly back down the hill, I paused by a large, old pine tree just to view the camp. I felt like I was waiting for something, but I didn't know what. I just wasn't ready to go back into the cabin yet. I had been deeply moved by both the Wisdom Master's words and the quality of her being. Earlier that day, I had filled out an application asking to become her apprentice, but I hadn't given it to her yet. She seemed so full of pure life force and a true, spiritual love for all those attending. I wanted to be sure that she was as real as she seemed.

Just then, on the periphery of my vision, something moved in the darkened camp below me—a whiteness or glow of some kind. I froze in place, and gazed steadily, trying to see what had caught my attention. Still dressed in white, the Wisdom Master stepped out soundlessly from between the trees and began to move among the cabins in the moonlight. Not a single sound betrayed her step as she slowly wove her way through the camp and its sleepers. She was luminous. Her movements were flowing and natural, but soundless, and it seemed she was literally walking in a state of deep meditation.

I was no stranger to large, group events, and I knew the effort it took to set up and run a week-long program such as we were part of...let alone, also to be the main speaker day after day. Yet here the Wisdom Master was in the wee hours of the night...moving among us with her blessing, even as we slept. And there I was in my bathrobe, peeping from behind a tree, whether I was supposed to see this or not, with my heart overflowing with gratitude.

As her form disappeared back into the woods on the other side of the camp, an explosion of joy shot through my being. I had found the Wisdom Master Teacher!

Divine Hearing

A small group of students were sitting with the Wisdom Master after a talk. We were informally discussing the morning's events. One senior student spoke of a project she wanted to undertake. I was new on the Path and not sure of myself in the community. When I heard the student describing this project, I arrogantly thought to myself, '*Well, I could do that kind of project and be just as good at it as she is.*' The Wisdom Master immediately turned to me and said, *"You be nice to her. She deserves your respect."*

My heart jumped into my throat, '*Oh, my gosh! The Wisdom Master heard my thoughts.*' I was awestruck at my Wisdom Master's power of perception and ashamed at the same time. From that point on, I realized that I could not hide from this Wisdom Master.

During Construction

The inside of the Stupa was sweet and cool as I left the hot summer afternoon outside. Through the arched doorway, which was still under construction, I could see a few apprentices lingering in the shade of the apple trees after completing the 2:00 p.m. Mantra chanting. Inside the sanctuary, I could no longer hear the singing of the insects; there was only silence.

Immersed in the peace I felt, I began to chant the Mantra, very softly at first. As the vibration of the sacred cadence filled me, I chanted more boldly and filled the chamber with the music that welled up from my heart. As I chanted, I thought of the Wisdom Master, and I realized that I had gone into the Stupa to be alone with Her presence.

The Stupa was filled with echoes, so that my single voice sounded like it rose from many lips. I reached out to the Wisdom Master with the love of my whole being and sang only for Her.

Then, as I turned, I *'saw'* the Wisdom Master standing in front of me smiling radiantly. She was dressed in her white robes of summer, and She stood in a glow of expanding love that filled me as I continued to chant even more loudly. Tears of joy ran down my face.

I noticed that the light in the Stupa suddenly changed. I looked over at the doorway. The Wisdom Master stood in white robes, illuminated by the summer light behind her. She smiled and walked over to the exact spot where I had previously 'seen' her stand in front of me.

"I heard you all the way down the walkway," She said.

I was so in awe, I could not speak. I had so yearned for her to be there, and there she was!

The next day at our 11:00 a.m. Teaching, we talked about 'arisings,' and I related my experience. The Wisdom Master said, *"I came to the Stupa because I was drawn by your love."*

    That summer day, I learned that by holding the Wisdom Master in my consciousness, with all the love that flows through me, she is with me always.

Double Delight

I was driving back with the Wisdom Master from a shopping trip to Kelowna, my first such expedition with the Wisdom Master. I had quickly learned to have no agenda, maintain a quiet mind, and just keep my attention glued on the Wisdom Master in companion energy. Following her through a store was like riding the tail of a comet! We were in; we were out; we were gone!

It seemed my only task was to keep my mind very quiet, relaxed, and attentive, move in harmony with her, and be of service in any way that might support what she was doing at the moment. I had discovered a great delight in simply doing that, along with a growing sense of open-ended freedom as I slipped into her way of 'moving and doing.'

It felt like anything might be possible, like we were moving 'through' time and space, but not within its confines. Everything we did was simple and yet filled with hidden potential. For me, it had turned into a grand adventure, a kind of 'divine play.' Moving in this spontaneous way, the day had been like a limitless, bright ribbon unrolling as we went—one happy find following another.

Now, as we neared Skycliffe, the Wisdom Master called ahead and asked one of the apprentices to drive up and meet us at Samadhi House to help us unload. After unloading, I said good-bye to the Wisdom Master, and leaving the Wisdom Master at her home, which is a mile away from the HÜMÜH parking lot, I rode back down to Padma Valley with the apprentice who had helped us unload. On the drive down the hill, I reflected on the day's events, wondering what it might be like to live and act from the Wisdom Master's freedom all the time, without the 'confines' of my own habitual, limited way of thinking and acting.

As we arrived in the parking lot, there was the Wisdom Master already standing inside the Padma Valley gate smiling at us! A chill went up my back. She was now wearing her robe, her hair was freshly combed, she wasn't the least bit breathless, and a big smile lit up her face! Inadvertently, I looked over my shoulder, wondering if she could have driven down right behind us in her car, but her car was nowhere in sight. Even if she had, there hadn't been time for her to change clothes and freshen up. There certainly hadn't been time for her to do that and race down the back way over Amitabha Trail on foot and be there inside the gate ahead of us with not a hair out of place!

I glanced at my companion apprentice in astonishment. The Wisdom Master swung open the gate for us. *"Welcome to Skycliffe!"* she said, and her eyes were dancing with Light. Gazing at her in awe and with my heart hammering gratefully in my chest, I stepped through that gateway and stammered, *"Thank you for a most wonderful day!"*

"You are very welcome," she replied. *"Go on in."* Little by little, I've been *going-on-in* ever since.

Ian Meets the Wisdom Master

When Ian Alexander turned three-years-old he decided to go to Skycliffe, and so he did. That's the way Ian was; when he decided to do something, he just did it. He took his mother and brother along with him.

When he first arrived, he found everything to be pretty agreeable—after all, everyone thought he was so cute and loved whatever he said. Yes, life was good this way at Skycliffe—that was, until the second day. That was the day he met his Teacher, Wisdom Master Maticintin, again.

Everyone had gathered at the Stupa, and a woman wearing a white robe came out and sat under an umbrella. This woman struck Ian as different, so he went to explore. He circled around the pole of the umbrella trying to understand. He came close to her, then moved farther away, then closer, then farther away, and so on. He felt a resistance towards this woman, and as the days went on, he acted out that resistance. It was as though, in the remembering of resistance from a past life, he began to repeat it.

When the white-robed Wisdom Master spoke to him, he turned his head away and pretended to ignore her. Yet at the same time, there was a struggle growing inside him. Part of him demanded that he resist; the other yearned to embrace the divine consciousness. As his mother watched in the days that followed, she wondered if he was too young to be able to handle his conflict.

Eventually, his resistance began to wane and he began to speak to this figure everyone else called 'the Wisdom Master.' His struggle was far from over, however, as old habits, seemingly from another lifetime, soon returned.

One day, Ian and his mother came out of the dining hall. They turned to see the Wisdom Master standing up on the Temple porch. She smiled and said, *"I would like to meet with you later."* Then she demonstrated to Ian how to bow and asked him, *"Can you do this?"*

This was the last straw for Ian. How dare she expect him to bow to her! *"Can you do this?"* he shouted back and threw down the jacket he was holding onto the dirt.

The Wisdom Master replied, *"I guess we wont be meeting today,"* as she turned and went back into the Temple.

Then there was the morning Ian was out in the orchard talking in a rather loud voice, even after several attempts from others to get him to quiet down. The Wisdom Master came out from among the trees, startling Ian.

"Ian," she said, *"You think you are the only one out here. Your voice can be heard all over the grounds. Keep your voice down!"*

Ian was completely thrown off balance. This woman corrected him, yet there was absolutely no emotion there for him to latch on to. He just stared at her as she turned and left in the same way she had come. Ian spoke in a voice barely above a whisper afterwards.

Just before lunch that same day, he was sitting on the porch outside the dining room, and the Wisdom Master came up to him again and said, *"You are a most disrespectful boy!"* as she went inside.

Ian just said, *"Huh?"* as he peeked at her through the window.

Now, she definitely had his attention. He watched for her all day. He listened for her voice and looked for her everywhere he went. The desire to let go of the resistance and open his heart continued to grow stronger.

That night as he climbed into bed, very tired after a long day of struggle, he told his mother, *"I'm going to be a super man."* His mother smiled because she knew that's the way Ian was. When he decided to do something, he just did it.

He began the next morning. His mother showed him how to bow and explained that to bow to another was an act of reverence to the divine consciousness that resides in everyone. Ian quickly caught on, and bowed to all he saw—that is, until later that morning, when his resistance was tested once again.

The Wisdom Master came walking along the road toward Ian as she was talking with another student. Ian saw her approach and walked by with his head down. *"Ian!"* his mother said, and he turned and quickly bowed to the Wisdom Master, but it was too little, too late. She had already passed.

Before lunch that day, he sat on the porch, watching for her to arrive. As soon as he saw her coming down the drive toward the kitchen, he jumped out of his chair, ran over to the edge of the porch, bowed to the Wisdom Master, then ran back and sat down with the others on the porch.

During lunch, he ate quietly. As he was finishing, he did a most amazing thing. He sang in a loud voice, calling out the name *'Vairocana,'* the Primordial Buddha of Wisdom. His heart had opened, and a few minutes later, he slipped away from his chair to go sit with the Wisdom Master, the person he referred to from that point on as *'my Wisdom Master,'* and they ate their first of many delicious desserts together.

A Light on a Dark Spot

When choosing to share this teaching story, the first thing that came to me was that my entire life with the Wisdom Master is a teaching story. When my attention is on the Wisdom Master, all my experiences open into opportunities to learn, to serve, and to take one more step closer to awakening.

Once, during a short, five-day retreat in December, the day before I was to leave, the Wisdom Master called me into her office. She was at her desk as I sat down on her couch. I remember feeling pretty good and thinking that perhaps the Wisdom Master was about to tell me that I was on track and doing well.

However, the Wisdom Master did not call me into her office to chat about how fabulous I was. Instead, the Wisdom Master asked a simple question of me. She asked when I was going to be rested? I didn't have a clue as to what she was talking about. I was sleeping like a baby in my snug room at the Log House. The Wisdom Master went on to say that I was making myself tired and that if I didn't do something about it, I was going to get diagnosed with Chronic Fatigue Disorder or some other disease related to constant fatigue. She went on to say that I needed to do something about this *now*. I don't remember the exact words, but I do remember the feeling...the penetration of her energy. It was like a light was being shined on this dark spot in my life. It suddenly hit me: I was indeed tired, deeply, deeply tired. Life was exhausting me; I didn't even see it.

The Wisdom Master's words echoed through me, and things started to come to the surface. I realized that I was tired because I wasn't 'giving'...I wasn't acting for the whole. I was acting for my little self. Life was tuckering me out because I was doing things that

I felt I 'should' and because I wanted to 'please' others. I started to see that I didn't necessarilyhave to stop everything in my life, but I had to change my approach. An internal shift arose--

In the weeks that followed, I started to look at my work as a service—not just as a way to earn an income. Instead of trying to make a project go the way 'I' wanted, I just let go and let myself be open. I realized I got exhausted when I was feeling one thing and doing another—in other words, when I wasn't aligning my actions with my dreams, stress and fatigue were sure to follow. I began to visit my parents when I felt relaxed and open to visiting, meaning I was visiting them because I loved them—not because I felt I 'should.' Suddenly, I had plently of energy for whatever was needed in the moment. The Wisdom Master speaks often of flexibility, spontaneity. I was starting to see that the more I could open, the more I could give, and the more I could stay available to serve in whatever way was needed.

The reason I chose to share this Teaching is that, although the actual moment that the Wisdom Master spoke to me was several years back, it still lives with me everyday of my life. Today, if I get tired, I know it is usually because I am serving myself. Then I remember the Wisdom Master, and I try to let go and pray to be of service to the whole. It is a reminder in my life that every moment with the Wisdom Master is a gift, and if I can take that moment into my heart, it will expand and continue to bloom in my life and, in that way, uplift the whole.

Moment with the Wisdom Master

I had just returned to Skycliffe and met the Wisdom Master on the grounds. She asked how my trip had gone, and I eagerly told her about the eagles, bear, moose, and hawks that I had seen along the way. She listened patiently, and then smiled gently and said, *"My, you entertain yourself well."*

Happiness Is a Choice

I was intending to live at the Skycliffe Monastery as soon as the housing was ready. However, it was not to be.

Wisdom Master Maticintin told me, *"I cannot allow you to move onto the property because you enjoy suffering. The energy of your suffering would impact everyone."*

Initially, I resisted what she told me, but deep inside, I knew that it was true. There was bitter-sweetness in suffering because it was so familiar to me. But it was such a crushing blow in those days to be told that I had to give up my dream of residency on the property. Worst of all, I had no idea how I could drop this bad habit. It was so old and familiar to me that it felt like the normal way to be.

The Wisdom Master said, *"It is a choice. You can put your attention on happy and beautiful images when you catch yourself suffering, or you can continue to look at those things that cause you to suffer."*

This meant I had to put a smile on my face even though I was not feeling like smiling. I fought within myself to push away any thoughts and fears that caused suffering in me. But it was not working. I gave myself a terrific headache and felt helpless. Then the Wisdom Master called me to her office and said, *"What is wrong with you?"*

I told her, *"For the first time in my apprenticeship, I am afraid my difficulties are too big for me to overcome. I feel totally helpless to free myself from this habitual suffering."*

Gently, she said to me, *"If you do not give up on yourself, I will never give up on you."*

"You will never give up on me?" I asked

"No, never," she replied.

Her words gave me strength right then and there. I felt strength starting to grow in my body. I felt I could do it.

For the next months, I most diligently put into practice what she told me to do. I put my attention on happy and uplifting things, chanted the *Wish-Fulfilling Gem Mantra* and the *Mantra for the Resolution of Karma* numerous times every day. After a time, I came to a point where I knew that I would be all right. I also experimented with my attention. I had enough control by then to put my attention back and forth on misery and on happy thoughts to see how it changed my feelings. I came to learn that, indeed, being happy was a choice.

Walls

One day, Wisdom Master Maticitin commented on the wide-eyed, innocent look I often had on my face. She added that when I looked that way, she knew I was "up to something."

I reflected on what she told me. I realized that my expression was a habitual way of protecting myself, not wanting to be exposed, even though I did not think I had any plans brewing. I saw that my expression was a form of withholding, and I knew I did not need this look with the Wisdom Master, as she saw me anyway. In that moment, I was grateful for the freedom she was offering me to tear down the walls and just be myself.

Aligning My Actions...

When we moved to Skycliffe, most of the residences were not ready, so a few of us stayed in cabins about forty minutes away. After a month or so, I was yearning to get into my new home at Skycliffe, and I expressed my frustration to Wisdom Master Maticintin. I remember that she told me to move in anyway, in order to get the energy moving, even though the bathroom fixtures were not yet hooked up. I was taken aback at first, but moved in the following day, and, wonder of wonders, the bathroom was functional the day after! I learned a little more about 'aligning my actions with my dreams.'

The Mirror Stands Tall

Several years ago, the Wisdom Master wrote an article titled, "*The Mirror Stands Tall Against the Energy of the City*." I was always very excited when a Teaching arrived and since I was living in a large city at the time, I was eager to see what my Wisdom Master had to say. I read the article and thought it was interesting and that it would probably mean more to others who get caught up in city energy and were more cynical than I. Yes, I liked living in the city, but I didn't find it energizing to be out among the crowds, and I didn't take part in many of the city activities. However, I decided, since every Teaching must have something to say to me, I would read the article again. As I did, I started seeing ways that I was attached to living in the city. I would tell friends that even though I didn't do many city activities, I liked that they were available. I started to see ways that I feared being without the structure and distractions of the city. Even when I spent time in the large park near my home, where I was often the only one, or one of a very few people there, I still was surrounded by the city and felt a comfort in that.

I wrote to the Wisdom Master about my initial response to the article and shared some of what I was now seeing about myself. I told her I was now reading the article with me in the mirror instead of my neighbors. She wrote back thanking me for my consideration of the article and for realizing that she was speaking directly to me.

We talked some time later about my experience, and I suddenly found myself committing to move out of the city. It is difficult to describe that moment. The Wisdom Master was not asking me to leave the city, nor had I even been debating that possibility myself. It seemed that my willingness to take a second look at the article, to open to what the message was for me, accessed a space for the experience to happen. In a moment of openness and complete trust in the Wisdom Master, I released my attachment to living in the distracting energy of the city. It was an experience unlike any I had ever had. It was devoid of any analyzing, any weighing of pro's and con's, any fear or 'what about's.' It was a moment of knowing, directly, what I wanted and spontaneously choosing it – a moment when my entire being was in alignment. When I sat with the experience, I knew it was not one of those decisions made in the emotion of the moment, because there was not a moment of regret or questioning of my decision, then or later. I saw that when the Wisdom Master shines a light on something that is a roadblock on my trek to enlightenment, if I am open, not in resistance, I can know what I want to do and choose to move in new directions with no fear.

Long-Term Resident

It was a few days before I would go back home for a month to pack
up and sell or give away my belongings before moving to Skycliffe
as a resident. I had talked to Wisdom Master Maticintin before, and I
knew she wanted me to 'stay longer,' but suddenly, I became insecure
about what that really meant. Here I was going to get rid of almost
everything that I owned, perhaps only to find out that maybe I was
only to stay for a year, and I had misunderstood it all.

So, when I had a chance to walk with the Wisdom Master for a
short distance, I asked her if she really did see me as a 'long-term'
resident at Skycliffe.

She looked me in the eyes and asked me in reply, *"Do YOU see
yourself as a long-term resident?"*

Without any hesitation, I answered, *"Yes."*

"Then so do I," was her response, as she walked away.

Although I did not fully understand it right away, over time, I
am learning and am experiencing more and more: I truly am the
dreamer of my life!

Being Lazy

During a conversation with Wisdom Master Maticintin, she told me I was lazy, and that it could hinder my spiritual progress. *'Lazy? Me Lazy? Oh, no, doesn't she know all the things I do?'* My mind went on and on trying to discount what had been said. When I was able to set aside my little-self fears of not being worthy and my pride being hurt, I began to see what had been said was true. I was inconsistent in my spiritual practice, doing it when it was convenient and not catching myself when I wandered in attention. I was not practicing keeping my attention on what I wanted. A spiritual life requires constant romancing.

Living What I Know

When I became a student of Wisdom Master Maticintin, there
was little sharing about that with my parents and siblings;
only the closest sister knew. When visits were scheduled with the
Wisdom Master, nothing was said other than that I was taking a trip.
It was only when questions or interest was shown that information
was shared.

Family realized things were changing, especially as the visits
increased in frequency and duration. When I could talk about truths
without labels or titles, conversations increased. This included communicating with my three children, two of whom are Jehovah Wit-
nesses.

Teaching in a large urban school district posed many challenges
and opportunities for me to live what I was learning spiritually. This
was exciting since I enjoyed working with the students and seeing
their growth. Gradually, over the years, teaching became more of a
challenge and a chore. Both student and parent attitudes towards
education and learning became more negative and confrontational. I
had always said it would be time for me to leave teaching when I was
no longer having fun. Yet I hesitated to leave, concerned about retiring early and how much money I would receive. When a fight occurred outside my classroom, I closed my door to protect the students
inside and called security. I could feel the energy of the situation, and
it pulsed within me, giving me a headache. Communicating with the
Wisdom Master about that situation, she indicated that when something like that happens, it may mean it's time to go. *"Oh, no, I can't
go now,"* I said to myself. As the weeks passed, and the school environment became more volatile, I realized she was right. So I started

the retirement process. Everything went smoothly, and when the pension amount was calculated—*surprise*—it was more than I had anticipated. *'Hey, I can do this.'*

But what would I do after retiring? The city energy was not conducive to my spiritual growth, so I asked about moving to the monastery. I was welcomed.

My mother was excited when informed of my retirement, but became quiet when told I was moving to Skycliffe. Later, came the questions about living arrangements and what would be provided for me versus what I was financially responsible for. My daughters railed against my leaving them. Parents were supposed to stay put. It was okay for children to move away, but not a parent. A sister questioned my driving abilities to pull a trailer half-way across the US and through the mountains. I told them I was doing something that would make me happy, and it would be nice if they could be happy for me.

But I wavered, concerned if I was making the right decision; then fear raised its head, and the more I mulled it over, the murkier the situation became. The Wisdom Master responded by saying she would love to have me here, but the choice was mine to make, and whatever decision I made would be fine with her. In my heart, it felt right, but my mind/head kept up the chatter of *'What about this or that?'*

Ignoring the mind chatter, I practiced staying focused on what I wanted— spiritual growth and moving to Skycliffe. When I put the attention on what needed to be done to accomplish the goal, the mind chatter diminished. My daughters realized the move was going to happen and decided to give me a going away party. I stated it was a 'moving' party. At the party, my mother told me she was proud of the way I lived my life. My brother asked numerous questions, and inwardly, I laughed, knowing he was being himself, trying to understand and find a way to give his approval.

I visited the family five months after the move, and there was joy in the reunion. The family saw I was happy. Going for what I want, living a spiritual life, is the greatest gift I can give them. I saw growth and vitality in my daughters. One is now taking her own new venture—preparing to open her own business.

Following Your Heart

W hen the Wisdom Master first introduced the *Wish-Fulfilling Gem Mantra*, we were taught one word at a time, and for a long while, we were only given the first stanza to chant. Our Mantra is a treasure and very powerful because it had not been used in a long time. It was a secret, and as new people came to visit, it was the Wisdom Master who introduced it to them when she felt they were ready. One day, with a new arrival present, the facilitator, who was a resident apprentice, began to chant the Mantra. The other apprentice and I who were there at the time looked at each other. We knew we should not be chanting the Mantra with a visitor present, but we did not know what to do. We chose the easy way out and did nothing.

The new arrival later asked the Wisdom Master about the Mantra. Soon after, the rest of us were called in to talk to the Wisdom Master. I said, *"Yes, I know it was wrong, but we did not know what to do."* She softened and explained it in a way that we came away with the feeling of *"Yes, we could have done that, if we had had the courage to follow our hearts."*

Art

All my life, I have had this strong interest in art. As I pursued different careers, it was always there in a corner of my life, but never taken seriously. A few years prior to moving to Skycliffe, I had finally taken some art classes at the college and enjoyed them. I continued to tinker around; but I also knew in my heart that I was not doing enough with it. There seemed to be fears holding me back, and I often felt 'not good enough' or not 'creative enough.'

Just before I came to Skycliffe, I had this 'revelation' through a dream, that I had been an artist in my previous lifetime and had ended up in a concentration camp during the 2nd World War. When I talked to the Wisdom Master about it, I asked her if there was any truth to this dream, which she confirmed, and why, if so, I was so blocked. What should I be doing about this 'art thing' that I had felt so strongly all my life but which I felt I wasn't living up to. The Wisdom Master didn't seem to want to elaborate more about my previous life, and I remember her telling me: *"Just be. Just be here at Skycliffe and be in the moment. You know – Art is all around you!"* and she waved her arm pointing in all directions.

Once the worry of who and what I 'should be' was eliminated and I just gave myself to doing what needed to be done, I began to truly see that art is, indeed, all around me. It is in the sweeping of the temple porch to make it look inviting, in the weeding of the Mandala Garden to beautify it, and in everything that I do when I give myself to the task at hand with appreciation for the essence in everything, its 'dharma nature.'

Interestingly enough, over time, the Wisdom Master began to give me more art and design-related jobs. My nervousness about 'not being good enough' is lifting with her encouragement and trust that I can do it. I am learning that it is not about 'being good' or 'not good,' but about how I can best serve the whole, always learning and stretching myself beyond my perceived limitations.

Domination or Liberation

Twelve years ago, I became bold and adventuresome. I chose the Wisdom Master as my spiritual guide. The early death of a life-long friend, the life-threatening illness of my husband, a dramatic health problem in my own life, all led me to ask myself, '*What is life all about? There is something more than what I see.*'

For eight years, I had been coming to Empowerments four times a year and several retreats a year while journeying through the Teachings. Then, in 2002, I decided all the circumstances in my life were prime for me to ask to become a resident of Skycliffe. I hadn't prepared my family well for my decision, so it was taken as a shock. My action was a dramatic step away from my old life, and it caused an equally dramatic reverberation in my family members.

I likened my moving to Skycliffe to leaping off a cliff blindfolded. I just knew I had to do it, or regret it for the rest of my life. Now here is where karma and habitual behavior followed me and showed up in spades. I was used to pleasing people, to having them like me, who I am and what I do. I needed approval. In fact, approval seemed linked to my emotional survival, and taken to the extreme, my physical survival. I tried to fit in to the Monastery routine and life and be happy, but always nagging in the back of my brain was, '*How come my family is so angry? Why don't they like me? I am a good person. Why are they treating me this way? What can I do to get them to like me and get them to approve of my choice?*' I was dominated by these thoughts to the extent that there was a dark cloud hanging over me and over my place of residence all the time.

That whole year, Wisdom Master Maticintin patiently reminded me that I needed to let go and stop trying to get their approval. She

79

saw how I was suffering, and four times, she called me into her office to talk about my going back home; but each time I insisted that this was the only life I really wanted. Actually, my suffering said that what I really wanted was my family's love and approval more than a devotion to a spiritual life. So after fourteen months, the Wisdom Master called me in for the final time and said something like, "*You have to go back and finish this karma. Maybe it will take two weeks, maybe two years, or maybe the rest of your life. But you won't be ready to be here until you do. The good news is, if you clear up this karma in this lifetime, you won't have to come back to do it again.*"

I could barely breathe. I knew there was no way to talk her out of her decision this time. '*The rest of my life?! No, not that!,*' I thought inside my head. I didn't want it to be so, but I knew the Wisdom Master was right. I was stuck, and it was impossible to move forward spiritually until I cleared up this untenable situation with my family.

I went home for Christmas to prepare a place for me to move into. Then I returned to Skycliffe to pack up my car for the drive back. The only thing that saved me from going under was a thought the Wisdom Master left with me: "*You are on a mission,*" she had said. I thought, '*I can do this. I can clear up things with my family and be back at Skycliffe in no time.*' It now became an adventure. The Wisdom Master gave one stipulation—that I could not return for at least six months. '*Okay,*' thought I. '*Six months is not so bad.*' And so I began my adventure, *my mission.*

Clearing karma apparently was not a six-month job. In six months, I hadn't even gotten my family to talk to me. I did return to Skycliffe for a visit after the first six months, but it was clear I was still carrying the pain of my family. So back I went to California to try new tactics with slipshod results. Another visit to Skycliffe for a month, but obviously I hadn't cleared anything. I was still hanging on to how I thought things 'should' be. And again, back to California. One edge began to loosen its hold. That was my mother. I visited with her in the retirement care center every week. A mother cannot close her heart to her child for long. As I became more *real* with her, she began to open to me, and we re-established a loving relationship. One brother also opened to me, and we had more honest conversations than we ever had before. But I wanted *all* my siblings to love me. There was the problem. I was not willing to let them be who they wanted to be and live their lives the way they wanted to live. I wanted it *my* way. I wanted me to be a part of their lives in a certain way. That wasn't what they wanted. And so, the more I pushed in one direction, the more they pulled away. Action/reaction.

It took me literally two years to the day to realize that it was always up to me, not my family. It was up to me to be willing to follow my destiny--to follow what I truly wanted--the only decision that would uplift everyone involved, because what I truly wanted was to follow my heart, first and foremost. I needed to let go of being a victim, to let go of trying to change other people, to accept and respect my family members' decisions to lead their lives the way they chose. The result has been ever-increasing freedom, liberation and joy. The Wisdom Master gladly welcomed me back as a resident of Skycliffe once she had seen that I learned what I needed to learn. I had accomplished my mission.

Wisdom Master

Once

When I was having
A
Difficult time,

The Wisdom Master looked into me
With
Endless Eyes

"How many steps are you going to take?"
She said

I looked into the
Whiteness all around us…

"One step at a time,"
I said.

"That is the correct answer,"
She replied.

Persevering

In the early years of HÜMÜH, Wisdom Master Maticintin held Gatherings throughout North America. When the Gathering was held in Kentucky, a few of us arrived early to assist the Wisdom Master in finalizing the arrangements and grooming the park for the event. As I remember it, the Wisdom Master walked the grounds, looking for the perfect place to hold the Gathering. She finally said that it would not do that it did not afford the privacy that we were promised when we made the reservations. Those of us with her were dismayed.

She then said that the only thing to do was to go to the park office, and talk to the people in charge of booking. Three of us who were with her got into the car, and we drove to the office, where she firmly explained the problem. The woman she was talking to was quite resistant, assuring us that there was no solution to our concerns, and not being open to a solution at all. The Wisdom Master then asked if there was someone else we could talk to, and another woman came out of an inner office.

When this woman heard what the problem was--lack of seclusion, being open to the public, etc--she thought for a moment and then told us that there was a field, adjacent to the campground but not frequently used in conjunction with it, that might prove to be the answer. She invited us to have a look and gave us directions. After the Wisdom Master thanked her, we went to check it out.

It was a short walk adjacent to the campground, but opening up into a wide, hilly field surrounded by trees, and with an old vine-covered building sitting to one side. The Wisdom Master announced that it would be perfect—with a little help. We got a crew together to clean up the site and arranged things so that the Wisdom Master could sit with her back to the vine-covered building, with the knoll rising in front of her, like an amphitheatre, where we could sit. On the top of the knoll, we placed a small stupa, containing the Teachings.

It was a perfect place. One evening, it became the site to take Bodhisattva vows, beneath a huge, luminous moon that illuminated the stupa on the crest of the hill. It was magical.

I learned that day about not settling for anything less than what you want, about persevering until a satisfying outcome results. We could have been in a cramped area with a public road running just to the back of us and the public eye upon us. Instead, we enjoyed a perfect, secluded space, and a wonderful experience.

An Impeccable Choice

This past January, I received word that my beloved great-uncle was terminally ill and had been admitted into hospice care. He had always been a central figure in our small, close-knit family, but having lived to the impressive age of 99, his impending death did not come as a surprise. Having lived most of life in close proximity to my family, I rarely missed family events, and at a moment's notice, I could visit a sick relative or lend a helping hand in some way. But now, living at Skycliffe, I was more than 2,000 miles away, and we were about to begin a Transcendental Awareness Class that I did not want to miss. Consequently, the decision of whether or not to fly back home to see my uncle one last time took some consideration. As I looked at this situation, I could feel the habitual energy start to kick in. It showed itself as an urge to immediately fly home just because that's what I had always done in the past, and perhaps my family would expect it, or I expected it of myself. But this time, I wanted to do things differently. I could see that to follow the habitual path would be to go against my heart. My heart wanted to be at Skycliffe, and intuitively, I felt that I could be of more help to my uncle in his time of transition if I stayed at Skycliffe. However, I wasn't sure exactly what I could do to be of service to my uncle and to have some closure on our relationship, without making the trip.

At that point, I spoke with Wisdom Master Maticintin about the situation in order to gain a fresh perspective from the overview. The Wisdom Master suggested that I spend a few hours composing a heartfelt letter to my uncle, recounting fond memories of him and expressing gratitude for what I had learned from him. Then, I could e-mail the letter to my brother and have him read it to my uncle at his bedside. I followed the Wisdom Master's suggestion and wrote the letter, but before it was completed, I received word that my uncle had passed away. Undaunted, I completed the letter. Later that evening, it occurred to me that I could still e-mail the letter to my family and ask that it be read at the funeral service. This idea truly resonated with my heart as a way to participate in the service without being there physically. Writing the letter had been such an uplifting experience that I was at peace with my decision not to attend the funeral. By writing the letter, I had been able to express my gratitude and prayers for my uncle's happiness in a way that left my heart feeling very full. As it turned out, my family was very understanding about my not being able to attend the funeral, and they were also receptive to the idea of having the letter read at the service. In fact, my cousin readily volunteered to do the reading.

After the funeral service, I heard from several family members who said they were touched by what I had to say, and they felt it was a fitting tribute to a man who had meant so much to our family. While I appreciated the positive feedback, I felt the most important part of this experience was that, with the Wisdom Master's guidance, I was able to follow my heart and truly act for the good of the whole. Had I traveled back to my hometown, I doubt I would have taken the time to write such a letter. Very likely, I would have been caught up in the busyness of family gatherings and lost sight of the purpose of the trip: to honor the memory of my uncle. By remaining at Skycliffe, everyone had benefited. I was able to keep my commitment to my spiritual goals, and at the same time, share my heart with my family.

Earthworms

It was a beautiful morning. After breakfast, Wisdom Master Maticintin suggested we take a walk along the beach. The Wisdom Master was travelling on a speaking engagement, and another student and myself, had accompanied her. We were returning to the hotel from the walk by passing through the parking lot, when the Wisdom Master found a worm on the asphalt. To protect the worm, the Wisdom Master picked it up and placed it in the dirt near the edge of the parking lot. Once the first worm was seen, others became apparent, and we spent several minutes returning them to the dirt. When I located a worm that appeared dead, the Wisdom Master said to remove it, too; earthworms are made from dirt, and when placed in the dirt, they return to life; and it did.

What's Wrong with This Picture?

On the second day of my first retreat with Wisdom Master Maticintin, I fell ill in the morning. The Wisdom Master suggested that I lay down in the warmth of the spring sun on an air mattress placed on the grass near her office, so that I could rest and take it easy until I felt better.

As soon as I was settled, the Wisdom Master asked if she could get me anything or do anything to make me more comfortable. I said I was fine, and she left, only to reappear over and over again, each time to make sure I was comfortable or to see if I needed anything.

Throughout the morning, she would walk all the way down the hill to check on me and walk all the way back up the hill to her office afterwards. She brought me books to read, returned with vitamins and water to help me get better, came back again and again just to check on me or to see if I needed more pillows, a blanket, or anything else. To me, this was wonderful; how thoughtful and kind of her to care for me.

For hours, back and forth, the Wisdom Master went, making sure I had everything, that I was well fed, had lots to drink, and something to pass the time away with. In between her taking care of me and running for things to make me comfortable, we had an occasional chat about anything and everything, as if we had been friends for years; it was great, and I enjoyed the attention.

The morning soon turned into afternoon. She came down the hill to see if I wanted something to eat, or needed more water, or anything at all. I made a half-hearted attempt to say I could get my own food, to which she responded, *"No, you rest, and I'll get you something to eat."* As she left, I settled back down to enjoy the warmth of the sun while thinking how nice it was for her to prepare a lunch for me.

After lunch, I was starting to feel a little peculiar about everything. Something was not right, but I couldn't quite catch it. I watched her trek back up to her place carrying away my dirty glasses/dishes, and realized how many times she had gone up and down that hill just to make me comfortable. It was with that thought that I felt a stirring sensation, the kind you get when coming out of a deep sleep, not quite awake and not quite asleep. As my eyes followed her back up the hill, I suddenly realized *I wasn't sick! When did that happen? Was I even sick after I told her I was?* I sat there stunned, saying over and over again, '*What is wrong with this picture? Why is the Wisdom Master waiting on me and going to all this trouble? Why am I letting her? Why did I get sick; when did I get better? I'm really, really missing something important.*'

My constant chattering was interrupted by a voice; the Wisdom Master was calling to me. I looked over to see her standing on her deck. There was so much light and ... something else coming from her, something I didn't quite recognize. She was asking if I wanted to see the pictures of the first Sedona Empowerment. I said, "*Yes, I'd love to.*" Then, I hurriedly looked around saying, '*Something is really wrong here; I have to get up, something is not right. Wait a minute. Why was I okay when she just called me, and now I'm not? Did she know I was in trouble? Did she do all of this for a reason? Why? What am I missing???*'

Slowly, very slowly, a sense of 'knowing' was working through my fog. It was not in words; it was in images of my arrival and first day with her. From those images, I somehow understood what was happening and why it was happening. I had arrived with a defensive, arrogant wall, filled with cynicisms, doubts and fears, along with many expectations of what was going to happen or not happen. I could see how I had closed out the Wisdom Master and how her wisdom had found a way to reach me.

She came and sat down next to me; her nearness surrounded me in a bubble of light and love (it was the feeling I didn't recognize when I saw her on the deck. It was love, a type of love I had never known. It was freeing, joyful, and unconditional. All thought instantly left me. We enjoyed the pictures together, talked about the Empowerment and other things. Afterwards, we sat quietly, and I turned to her and said, *"I'm feeling better now."* She looked deeply at me for what seemed like a long time and said, *"Yes, you do!"*

The Wisdom Master, by waiting on me hand and foot, provided an act of love that allowed me to experience the true feeling of unconditional love and to see how much control my arrogance and pride had on how I lived and viewed my life. It was a joyful and humbling experience, a gift of pure love from the Wisdom Master.

A Visitor from Japan

One day, Wisdom Masters Maticintin asked me, *"Do you think your mother would like to come to Skycliffe for a visit?"*
And this led to my 83-year-old mother's visit to Skycliffe all the way from Japan. She was concerned about the language barrier at the Canadian airport, so I went to Japan to fetch her.

When I brought her to Skycliffe, she was shy at the beginning. She did not know the language, and she did not know anyone else but me. But, soon, she started to feel relaxed and happy. The Wisdom Master made her feel very welcome, and everyone was kind to her. She often visited the prayer wheel at the Stupa and wrote prayers, put them in the prayer wheel, and turned it with such heartfelt sincerity, almost hugging it with both hands. I was very touched to see her that way.

She wanted to participate in our work, so I asked her to help me with mailing: putting the labels on, sorting, stuffing the envelopes etc. She also helped in the creation of the coloring book, *Humuhscapes*, and swept the downstairs floor every day. She had become one of us for the duration of her visit.

She attended the teaching in the Temple every day when the Wisdom Master gave a talk. She did not understand a word of what the Wisdom Master was saying, but she seemed to be taking it in energetically. Her remarks often surprised me, because they showed the depth of her insight into what the Wisdom Master was conveying to us.

When she sat at the Mantra chanting sessions, she would trace the words in the book with her index finger as we chanted, singing the *Wish-Fulifilling Gem Mantra* softly. Again, her sincere bearing touched me.

The Wisdom Master observed her and said that my mother had a good heart, and that she was wholehearted. This was a bit of a surprise to me. I suppose I had taken her for granted all these years. But this opened my eyes, and I could see her in a more appreciative manner. Yes, it is true; she has a good, big heart, and she is wholehearted in all she does. I remember her re-doing something many times until she was satisfied. I often used to think that she was wasting her time and energy. What a small person I had been not to be able to appreciate her wholeheartedness!

My mother and I took a walk almost every day. With our long walking sticks, we knocked the snow off tree branches to lighten the weight of the snow. We were like little kids playing in the snow and ventured deeper into the woods. The sight of deer delighted her. She had never seen a wild deer in her life.

She enjoyed the monastery meals as well. In fact, she seemed to be enjoying everything. She perked up, her face glowed, and I was surprised at the vitality she was feeling in herself. When she saw the Wisdom Master, her face visibly brightened with joy. I wondered to myself, *'Maybe she has been a Wisdom Master's student in past lives?'*

Initially, she was to stay at Skycliffe for a month. The Wisdom Master wanted her to stay longer, so, she happily stayed for another month. I could feel my mother's feeling of joy when she received the invitation from the Wisdom Master.

My mother and I did many things together: watching video movies, taking walks, shopping, cooking, and chatting about important and not-so-important things. She said to me, *"I am so glad that I came. Now that I have seen the place and met the people, I don't have to worry about you any more."* What a load off my shoulders it was to hear that, and my shoulders physically relaxed.

Thus, the days went by very quickly, and the day came to say good-bye to everyone and to Skycliffe. As we drove past the outside gate, my mother looked back one last time and said good-bye aloud. She had never felt so accepted and appreciated for who she was. She was a contented person, and she was happy for me for the life choice I had made to live at Skycliffe.

A Treasured Gift

As I approcahed my house one July evening after meditation, I saw Wisdom Master Maticintin sitting on the porch steps. I took a deep breath uncertain of what the visit meant. As I got closer, I saw that wonderful smile of hers, and I relaxed.

At first I did not see the carrier at her feet. She reached into it and came out with a three-month-old male, tabby kitten and handed him to me. I was overwhelmed with joy as I held him. My nineteen-year-old tabby had died in November, and though I had determined to not have any more animal friends, that notion flew right out my mind when I held him in my arms.

He has been extraordinary in any number of ways. From the start, he had a stance and a presence unlike any other cat, with behavior to match. Then one day, I made the connection between what I was seeing and the Teachings on how we find mirror images of ourselves in our environment.

When this little guy wanted to do something, he wanted to do it *now*, in his own way, and he didn't brook much interference from anyone. *'Hah, who else do I know with a stubborn streak? Could it be me?'* As I continued to watch the triggers for his behavior, I began to see more of myself, and the 'oops' and the 'aha' of it all began to penetrate my awareness.

When he was thwarted from doing what he wanted, he had an immediate reaction. He ran across the room into the bathroom, literally threw himself against the bathtub, then propeled himself back into our living space, hitting the opposite wall. Finally, he went to his scratching post and gave it a good going over. *'Hmmmm, was he upset about something or was he mirroring something in me?'* I could see the relationship between what I was feeling and his reactions.

Each day I continue to learn more and more about myself in the reflections of my cat—a treasured gift from the Wisdom Master in more ways than one!

Peonies

I came out of the Temple after the evening sitting. I was in a good space; my mind was unusually quiet. The Wisdom Master and some other apprentices were admiring some flowers in front of the Temple. The Wisdom Master said that I should see the flowers, so I walked over and looked at them, even smelled one. They were very beautiful, and I appreciated the Wisdom Master's sharing them, but I didn't really understand why she had pointed them out. The next day, the quiet faded from my mind somewhat as the mind chatter began to return, but when I looked at those flowers, I could go back to that quiet space of the day before. Thank you, Wisdom Master Maticintin.

Mindfulness Bowl

To help us develop mindfulness, Wisdom Master Maticintin gave us each a small glass bowl filled to within ¼ of an inch of the top with water. We were instructed to carry it with us wherever we went. At first, it sounded like a novel idea and perhaps even fun, but soon the novelty wore off as water began spilling everywhere, indicating that I had fallen out of mindfulness. My little self, however, did not want to be reminded that I was not being mindful. I started looking at the bowl as a major inconvenience instead of a gift from the heart of the Wisdom Master. Instead of admitting my frustration, I stuffed the feelings and told myself that I would just put up with it for the next few weeks. A few days later, I *accidentally* dropped the bowl, and it broke into a number of pieces. I stared at the ground in disbelief. As much as I had disliked carrying the bowl around, I instinctively knew that dropping it was not a good sign. The next day, I confessed to the Wisdom Master that I had broken my bowl. She told me she wasn't surprised. The mindfulness bowl had revealed a pattern of stuffing anger and frustration that I had never wanted to own up to. A few weeks later, I was able to find a replacement bowl at the store. This time, I was more appreciative and open to what the bowl had to teach.

Resentment Crumbled

I was trying to change how I thought about my relationship with my boss and took this to the Wisdom Master. I felt hesitant because my thoughts were tarnished and mean-spirited. I also knew that, while I wanted to keep this meanness hidden from her, the only way to free myself was to be open...and, of course, she knew of this energy that I had, even though I had not shared it before. She listened patiently while I complained, *"My boss never says, 'thank you;' rarely says, 'nice work;' and never acknowledges that I have done the work for which she received praise."* This litany of resentment was concluded by my whine, *"I feel used!"*

The Wisdom Master allowed a time to pass, looking into my eyes, and then replied, smiling broadly, *"But of course you do! You are serving, and therefore ARE to be used! That's what service is...that's what work is! You should be used."*

In that moment, I felt the 'resentment stone' around my heart crack and a sense of peace take its place. I could smile at the person from whom I had wanted praise instead of searching for how to contribute. This encounter took place years ago, and like many Teaching moments, it reached inside to touch the divinity within. The poison in my thoughts dissolved. It was replaced with a buoyant, heart-deep sense of gratitude. Imagine the privilege of work as an expression of the Divine Self! I return often to that Teaching...sometimes it's when there's a glimmer of incorrect thought, and always, I notice how wonderful it is to express work as living spritual practice.

Don't Look Back

I came to Skycliffe on retreat one summer on crutches. Several weeks before, a car accident had resulted in knee injuries that, in spite of rest and physical therapy, had not improved much. I hobbled around for a day or so before the Wisdom Master called me into her office.

As I remember, the light, which was always airy and bright in her office, seemed somehow subdued as I sat on the sofa facing her. She asked me what happens when I go home after visiting Skycliffe. I paused, knowing that I have difficulty maintaining the energy I feel here when I go home, even though I do my utmost to continue my spiritual practice. But, instead of explaining that, something else came unexpectedly out of my mouth. I told the Wisdom Master that my fear is that I will not help enough.

"Others?" she asked.

"Yes, others," I replied.

The Wisdom Master appeared to be looking very far into somewhere I could not see. Her words wove in and around me as she spoke. I remember that she related to me the story of Jesus when he said to put your hand to the plow and not look back. She told me not to look back. Then she stood up, saying that she hoped my knees would be better soon. I felt the words rush out of my mouth; *"They are better already,"* I said. The Wisdom Master smiled, and I left.

That afternoon, I left my crutches behind and started to walk on my own, sometimes with a little help from my husband for balance. Within a couple days, I was doing fine, working to regain muscle strength, beginning to focus on giving service by working in the kitchen.

I enjoyed my retreat immensely, feeling the loving guidance of the Wisdom Master, and allowing myself to be nourished by the Teaching, as I felt a new aliveness in me that grew every day.

Dream Interpretation

In an e-mail to the Wisdom Master, I wrote about a particular dream scene that I had experienced the previous night. I had dreamed that I had been back home in my parents' house, and I was talking to my mother in the living room. Suddenly, I became aware that it wasn't really my mom I was talking to, but Wisdom Master Maticintin. Then I woke up.

I did not know what this dream was telling me. Did I feel that my Spiritual Wisdom Master was assuming a 'motherly role' in my life, or was there another meaning to it? I asked her about it.

Her reply, as I remember it, was: *Your dream means that I am all people that you talk to, as long as your attention is on me.*

Ahhhh - what a beautiful revelation.

Vision Quest

Recently, the Wisdom Master recounted a memory of walking along a pathway with her teacher, Padmasambhava. Her story stirred a memory in me of my first vision quest. I had been out several days, and this was the final morning. I sat on the ground and watched through the low limbs of the surrounding fir trees as she approached across an open field of tall grass. There was so much dedication and resolve in the fully contained power of her stride, so much clarity of purpose, that I was very deeply moved just knowing her movements were directed towards me.

When she arrived, she sat down and asked me what the most significant event of my vision quest was. *"Watching you walk across that field,"* I said in a quiet voice, tears in my eyes, so grateful that someone had finally taken my spiritual training in hand.

Double Trouble

It seemed to me that Wisdom Master Maticintin looked for ways to bring us out of our shells so she could work with us. On a retreat, an apprentice had written about an experience that several people had had with the Wisdom Master. The Wisdom Master asked me to study the story, then tell it. For a few days, I labored to get the words memorized exactly as they were written on paper. Then one morning, the Wisdom Master asked me to relate the story to the group. I began telling the story almost word for word. When I had finished, the Wisdom Master thanked me but added that the telling had no life to it. It was true. I even bored myself. In wanting to be perfect, I wasn't natural.

She asked me to prepare to tell it again the next day. Then we all left the meditation hall, and the Wisdom Master went up to her office. The emotion of a sense of failure was building inside me until someone asked me how I felt. I broke down in tears, sobbing. Even behind the closed door of her office, the Wisdom Master could feel my outburst. She came out onto the porch and called me up to her office. *"Double trouble,"* thought I.

Hesitantly, I walked into her office where she was working at her desk. She asked me to sit down on the couch while she finished some paper work. I was still sniffling. The cat came over and rubbed against my leg. I said, *"Ahh, she is trying to comfort me."* The Wisdom Master said, *"She is just curious about the energy."* The dog lay on the floor just looking at me. Soon the Wisdom Master came over and sat in a chair kitty-corner from me. Then she asked, *"What's going on?"* I told her frankly what I was experiencing, talking through tears. She listened patiently, then said, *"Have you ever noticed how crying looks the same as laughing?"* I started to laugh through tears and said, *"Yes. My mouth turns up at the corners and my eyes get squinty when I am laughing or crying."* I can't remember what else was said, but I felt better.

The experience opened me up to my vulnerability which opened me to my naturalness. The next day, I told the story again, but from my heart this time.

How Near Is Near?

When my wife and I retired, we decided to move closer to Skycliffe so that we could seriously pursue our spiritual goals. We considered several locations that we felt would let us visit the monastery more frequently. At the time, there were two other important considerations: one, to purchase, instead of rent, a home; and two, to be close to our medical plan carrier to make sure that we would have medical coverage.

Within those mindsets, our first consideration was Portland, Oregon. The homes in that area were reasonably priced and our medical insurance plan would cover us there. We quickly realized, however, that the distance to Skycliff was way too far. Then we figured that we could always drive south to Portland to get medical care and looked at towns further north like Spokane and various small towns closer to the Canadian border. However, once again, we soon realized that a 3-4 hour drive, one way, and having to cross the border was too long on a regular basis, and we abandoned the northern Washington area and started looking at places inside Canada.

We discovered a new development in Grand Forks and briefly considered buying a small lot and then building our own new home on it, but that seemed like a lot of work. Then we found a beautiful three-story home outside Greenwood on a five-acre lot. Now we felt it was time to come up and take a closer look and talk to the Wisdom Master about our plans.

When I came to Canada to look at the Greenwood home, the realtor also showed us a home on the shores of Jewel Lake 25 minutes outside Greenwood, and I really liked the quiet, peaceful location right on a private lake.

That evening, I went to Skycliffe and stayed for the evening meditation. After meditation, I told the Wisdom Master that I had talked with my wife, and we were considering making an offer on the home on the lake. She studied me very carefully, and then recommended not to make an offer on that home. She said that an almost two hour, one-way trip to Skycliffe was far too much, and we might as well stay in California if we couldn't find a place closer. She also said that we should rent and not buy a home because we needed to simplify our lives and focus on our spiritual practice, instead of having to maintain and take care of a home. I listened carefully and brought the message home to my wife.

We followed the Wisdom Master's advice, and within three months everything came together for us. We sold our home, a rental became available in Westbridge, and we moved to Canada. We never get tired of the daily, short, scenic drive to Skycliffe.

What I have learned from this experience is the importance of eliminating mind sets, to be open to new ideas, and to trust the Wisdom Master and the divinity that already lives within us.

A Mud Puddle's Wealth

One day, I was sitting at my desk at home working on some papers when the phone rang. I answered, thinking it was a friend calling to make dinner plans. To my great surprise, it was the Wisdom Master. After saying hello and trying to calm myself, I heard her ask me how I was doing. Of course, in those days, I was always doing 'fine.' My world might be coming to an end, but, none the less, I was always, 'fine.' After a very brief conversation, the Wisdom Master said, *"Is there a mud puddle somewhere near your house?"* I was immediately on guard because such a question usually led to some new experience. I said that, in fact, there was a small marsh behind my house in a wooded area. The Wisdom Master told me to go sit in the mud puddle for an hour. Swallowing and trying my best not to let my mind run wild, I managed to say, *"Okay, I can do that."* She said good-bye and that we would talk later about the experience.

Well, by the time I managed to get my head around the fact that I was going to be sitting in a mud puddle in broad daylight in view of my neighbors, I had had quite the conversation with myself. I mean, it was one thing to do such strange behaviors at the Wisdom Master's residence where no one who knew me back home would be the wiser. But to do such strange behavior right in plain view of all my neighbors was unsettling, to say the least.

I finally found some old clothes to wear and headed for the puddle. I was thinking that at least it was in the middle of the day, and most of my neighbors would be at work. I was also grateful that the weather was mild so I would not be cold. Walking out back and climbing over a small fence, I began looking for a good puddle. By now, I had managed to calm myself and had adopted my 'Good Apprentice' mode of being. I was going to do this with no problem I told myself. Suddenly, in front of me was the perfect puddle--several feet across and about six inches deep. Sloshing to the middle, I plopped down and sat cross-legged facing my house.

As I sat there, I wondered why in the world, the Wisdom Master had asked me to perform such a task. I wondered, *'Could she be trying to shift my attitude?'* I continued to ponder this question when suddenly I noticed some movement in a window of my neighbor's house. *'Oh, great,'* I said to myself, *'that neighbor already thinks I am a bit strange, and this is going to be all over the neighborhood by nightfall.'*

But, I continued to sit and ponder, and suddenly, I started chuckling to myself at the absurdity of my situation. Looking back at the day, I realized that I had gotten caught up in staring at myself and my problems and was over-analyzing everything I touched. Then I saw that the state of 'fineness' I was proclaiming was actually quite miserable. Not only was the Wisdom Master trying to get me to shift my attitude, she was saving me from myself and my self-imposed misery. The longer I sat in that puddle, the funnier it all became. For the first time, I got to see a glimpse of the notion that life is a dream, and I am the dreamer. The Wisdom Master had been saying that to me for years. Sitting in that puddle that day, I saw it and realized that, while none of the circumstances had changed, my relationship to the circumstances was my choice. I also saw the value of taking absurd action to break the bond of the attitudes that sometimes bound me in knots. In the years to come, this lesson would serve me well.

By the time the hour was up, I was carefree and had a big smile on my face. All my concerns about what others might think were gone, and I was enjoying the day in a way that I would not have thought possible that morning. I rose from the puddle, walked to the edge, turned back and thanked the puddle for its gift to me. I also said a prayer to Wisdom Master Maticintin thanking her for her support. Little did I realize, prior to that day, the value and wisdom available in a mud puddle.

Outhouse Lesson

On Orcas Island, I took a day trip, with the Wisdom Master on a small boat to one of the other nearby islands that she wanted to explore. This island was a lush forest park with a trail going completely around the island. Well, when we arrived, I needed to make a trip to the outhouse. When I went in, I noticed that it was in good shape except for quite a bit of toilet paper on the floor...I didn't think much about it, finished what I needed to do, and ran back to where the Wisdom Master began to hike through the forest on the path that was provided. It was a magnificent hike, breathing in the air of the lush forest mixed with the warm ocean breeze...quite intoxicating.

When the hike came to an end, we both made a last trip to the outhouse before we got back on the boat. The Wisdom Master went first, and as she was coming out the door, I noticed her throwing a large wad of toilet paper into the trash can. I walked into the outhouse where I had previously seen all the toilet paper on the floor and was quite astonished when I saw that it was now all cleaned up...the Wisdom Master had cleaned it up! I was quite surprised when the Wisdom Master said to me, *"Always make things better for those that follow."* I was shocked and humbled by her action. I would have never even considered cleaning up the toilet paper in an outhouse like that...now I would do it in a heartbeat...and have done it...the humbleness of that experience always returns.

I learned that there should be no conditions to my service...I should always give wholeheartedly whatever would serve those that follow.

A Change in Perspective

After many encounters with Wisdom Master Maticintin, I am realizing that even the briefest conversation can create an expansion of consciousness, if one is open to it. The other day, we were talking about what time we were going to meet the next day. I found myself saying, *"If you **need** more time..."* She replied that she did not NEED anything. The way that she mindfully responded, reflected back to me how unmindfully I often say things.

The Sign

Skycliffe lay heavy in snow, but it felt like spring. The apple trees were adorned with fluffy, white 'blossoms' as they dreamed of summer fruit. As if to mirror the redecorated orchard, the dining room was bathed in a flurry of change. The Wisdom Master had ordered new tables, chairs, linoleum, and fabric for window coverings. Apprentices brought out the bright blue and white fabric and laid it on the table as the Wisdom Master explained how it would be cut to frame the windows.

We stood waiting expectantly. *"NOW!"* the Wisdom Master said. *"We will do it NOW."*

The energy in the room rose. Apprentices positioned boards on fabric as the Wisdom Master took scissors and made clean cuts designated by the pattern of the boards. Then, she took a hammer and, with swift, clean strokes, pounded the valences to the waiting window frames. When the first of the blue and white trim was in place, the kitchen took on a new glow.

Then, as the Wisdom Master noticed that the window ledges needed repainting to match the walls, she said, *"We will do it NOW."*

Suddenly, the paint and brushes appeared, and apprentices joined together in quiet companion energy to paint contentedly, as the room was transformed.

"How do you like it?" the Wisdom Master asked me as she sat framed by the soft, blue fabric.

"Beautiful," I responded, as I looked into her eyes and noticed how she lit up the room. Then I glanced up and over the Wisdom Master's head, and read the sign on the wall that had always been a powerful reminder for me. It read:

"The Moment a Decision is Made
THAT
Is the Moment to Act"

The sign seemed to be a perfect 'caption' for the scene I was viewing in the warm dining room. Then, I realized how the message on the wall had suddenly caught my attention in order to give me the nudge I needed as I made a decision on my spiritual path. There was something I needed to do. The sign was a SIGN.

Power of Attention

In the second year of my apprenticeship with Wisdom Master Maticintin, I visited her for a week at Skycliffe. In those days, I was suffering from right knee pain, which sometimes gave me a lot of discomfort, and I was aware of the pain all the time, every day.

My first visit was going rather well, and I was enjoying the serene quietness inside me that I had never tasted before. There was nothing earth-shattering, just nice and quiet, I thought to myself. To think back now, this fact in itself should have been earth-shattering to me. I was used to a busy, chattering mind that kept going non-stop. But, alas, such was the level of my awareness in those days, and I thought nothing much of it then.

However, I did observe one change. Toward the end of my stay, I realized that I had not had the knee pain for some time, days, in fact. This was really peculiar, and I wondered if the Wisdom Master had taken the pain away. So, just before my departure, I asked her, and her reply was, *"It's because, while here, your attention was not on the things that caused the pain in your knee."*

I could not quite understand it then, but this was the first glimpse into the power of attention for me.

The Shoes

One summer morning, I was watering the multicolored flowers that hung in large baskets on the porch of the Temple. Before I had begun, I had taken the Wisdom Master's shoes from their place outside the Temple door and placed them with utmost care under a bench so they would not get wet. When I had just about finished watering, the Wisdom Master came out of the Temple and looked around for her shoes. *"They are over here,"* I said. I walked quickly over to where they lay and picked them up to hand them to the Wisdom Master. As I moved towards her, however, in my awkwardness, one of the shoes fell to the floor with a deep thud. I quickly picked it up and handed it to her, saying that I was sorry. I remember that she smiled and said something about *"no harm done."* I had been at Skycliffe a few months, but was still in awe of the Wisdom Master. I was trying to do everything 'right,' and I so wanted to be helpful. I made a mental note to be more careful next time.

'*Next time*' came only a few days later. This time, when I reached for the Wisdom Master's shoes, I gave their transportation my full attention. Hardly breathing, I retrieved the shoes and handed them to the Wisdom Master as if they were Cinderella's slippers, made of glass. The Wisdom Master smiled and gave me a gentle look of understanding and said, *"They are not sacred, you know, just shoes."* The twinkle in her eye told me to relax, and I could see that I had been trying too hard. So, I smiled with her as I began to learn that to be truly helpful meant to open myself in trust.

Don't Get Stuck

One day, several apprentices, including myself, were working down by the horse barn. It had been an unusually heavy rainy season, and the ground was completely saturated. Pools of standing water were everywhere, and we were wearing knee-high boots to be able to walk without sloshing mud onto our pants. Each step was labored, because each time we placed one foot down, we sank about ten inches. The mud oozed around our feet and seemed to cling like little suction cups, holding our boots fast.

The Wisdom Master had asked us to depress trenches with our feet to allow the water to flow down to the big trench that went around the barn. City slicker that I am, she had to show me how to do it, demonstrating how I could place one foot in front of the other to depress the mud as I inched my way toward the main trench. Since there was a slight downgrade to the area, the trough made by my feet quickly filled up with water with each step I took. Of course, I couldn't help feeling that I was doing something wonderful, and so, naturally, I paused to admire my workmanship. However, when I tried to move my feet again, I realized that they had sunk even deeper into the mud, making it virtually impossible to lift a foot without losing a boot.

The Wisdom Master finished her trench-making demonstration, turned to walk away, then paused and said, *"Don't stand still too long, you might get stuck."*

Being Seen

On one Wednesday evening, I was one of those who phoned the Wisdom Master from home. In those days, I was still learning to be comfortable with Wisdom Master Maticintin. 'Comfortable' meaning being willing to be real, not pretentious. At one point I said, *"You know, Deepak Chopra says exactly the same thing as you do."* The Wisdom Master said, *"Why can you hear it from him and not from me?"* Without pre-thought, I responded, *"Because you can see me, and he doesn't."*

See-Saw, Anyone?

One day, Wisdom Master Maticintin and I saw a television show called *Xena*. In this particular episode, there were two people on a see-saw. After the show, almost instantly, the Wisdom Master and I talked about how much fun it would be to have a see-saw on the property.

Like two kids, we went outside in the early evening, placed a board over a large tree stump, and, well, we began to see-saw. Oh, what fun we had giggling, laughing, just having a blast. It was even funny watching the dogs because they were all looking at us with the same inquisitive look as if to say, '*What are they doing?*'

The next day, the Wisdom Master shared the idea of making a permanent see-saw on the property. In the Temple, the Wisdom Master asked, *"Can anyone here draw a see-saw?"* I said, *"I could,"* but before I got the word *could* out, the Wisdom Master asked that I hand another apprentice a pencil and paper to draw a see-saw. The apprentice said, *"I don't know quite how to do this, but I'll try."*

Assuming the Wisdom Master hadn't heard me before, I said, *"Wisdom Master, I can do it."* Emphatically, she responded, *"NO!"*

The other apprentice began drawing. I had a piece of paper under my mat, and while waiting for her to finish, I drew a very short sketch of a see-saw. When the apprentice finished her see-saw, she showed the Wisdom Master and the other apprentices in the Temple. The Wisdom Master said, *"It is not quite what I had in mind."*

I then showed her my drawing. The Wisdom Master looked at me and said, *"I did not want you to draw a see-saw. You and your little self—you want to control. You always want to control."*

"Shhhh!"

To say that I am a person who likes to be heard, who likes to give my opinion, who likes to be noticed, who likes to be liked, is an understatement. It is a habitual behavior that has *run* me and keeps me asleep to my actions. But it is a behavior easily noticed by the Wisdom Master.

One day in the Temple after a morning teaching, Wisdom Master Maticintin asked for comments or questions from those present. Of course, my hand went up. I had something that I felt was quite marvelous to say, but instead, the Wisdom Master called on others who gave their comments. Not being called on to speak, I then thought of something else I could say. My hand went up. She called on me. I commented. And then others made comments. '*Oh, yes,*' I thought in my mind. '*There is something else I can say.*'

As I raised my hand again, the microphone was passed to me. I put my mouth close to it to speak, but before I could speak, the Wsdiom Master said quietly, *"Shhh."* I returned her gaze with a look of wonderment. '*Does she want me to speak softly?*' Then she said again, *"Shhh."* With my mouth open, not saying anything, I began to put the microphone down, but my mouth followed the microphone as it inched its way toward the cushion in front of me. Again, in a most loving way, she said, *"Shhh."* Finally, the microphone touched the cushion, I released my grip on it, and the Wisdom Master sat back and said, *"Now, are there any other comments?"*

Romancing Your Job

I did not realize that I had been having some habitual feelings about my work and was feeling unhappy about it. Wisdom Master Maticintin told me that to change this I had to 'romance' my job and suggested I fix up my office so that it was pleasant to work there. This included having fresh flowers and good light. Then I was to take a photo of it and show her.

By the time I got finished doing that, my office looked really attractive--with flowers, and lighting, and pictures. I was happy to be there and happy to come to work. My co-workers noticed, too, and it was uplifting for them. Putting my attention on making it a nice place to work, made it a nice place to work.

Laughter as a Teaching Tool

Another student and I were leaving after spending two weeks with Wisdom Master Maticintin. She stood watching as we loaded our gear into the vehicle. I stumbled over my bags, had difficulty lifting and placing them in the vehicle, then tripped getting into the vehicle. When I looked at the Wisdom Master, she was laughing heartily. As we drove away, I wondered, *'Why the laughter?'* I realized that I was not focused on the task at hand—preparing to leave. I had split attention: going about the task of leaving, but thinking about what needed to be done once I was back home. Therefore, I caused the bumpy energy which resulted in the lack of coordination of my movements. The Wisdom Master's laughter enabled me to see how living habitually, in this case not being in the present moment, causes chaos and confusion.

Boxes

One evening while I was typing an article on my computer, I somehow hit a key that eliminated all the boxes that I normally use to effect commands. My 'print' box, my 'cut and paste' boxes, my 'save' box, and so forth, all disappeared. This had happened to me once before, but my computer-expert husband corrected it while I watched. This time, no matter how I tried, I was unable to reconstruct the boxes.

As I was in the process of fussing and becoming frustrated over my lost boxes, Wisdom Master Maticintin entered the room. *"What's going on?"* she asked me.

"All my boxes are gone," I complained.

"Good," she said emphatically.

At that moment, another apprentice who had come in to try and help me 'find my boxes,' looked up curiously at the Wisdom Master's comment.

Then the message struck home. All these years, she had been calling me the 'box lady.' She said I have mental boxes for everything. Now, symbolically, I had given up my boxes all at once. I laughed, and the Wisdom Master laughed with me, as she saw the message strike home.

Blue Prints

My analytical mind loves to figure things out and organize things. I am happiest when I have a blueprint, so that I know what and when things have to be done.

On many occasions, I have asked the Wisdom Master questions like: *"What happens next? After we finish this or that, what do we do then?"*

I always thought that detailed plans were essential before starting any project. Although the Wisdom Master admits that plans were needed for large projects like building the Stupa and Temple, this is not how she normally operates. The Wisdom Master has taught me that living in the now, being flexible, and doing things in the moment is far more important than having detailed plans.

I have found that by planning ahead as little as possible, my mind is a lot quieter, because it does not have to weigh all the options and possibilities. With a quiet mind, I am open to receive options that would have been blocked otherwise.

My awareness of this habit has been increased and a valuable lesson learned.

Courtesy Cover-Up

When I first came to Skycliffe, for a time, I lived in a room next door to the Wisdom Master's office. This was a great privilege. It afforded many opportunities for encounters with the Wisdom Master, and I cherished those occasions. What I sometimes found difficult was knowing when to make contact and when to allow the Wisdom Master her space.

Instead of simply opening my heart, being in Third Eye Vision, and discerning the timing spontaneously, ego often fell back on habitual behavior. My mother had trained me to always be polite, to say *'Hello'* or *'Good Morning'* whenever passing a neighbor or someone I respected, to stop and offer to pick up something from the store if I was going, to say *'Thank you'* anytime anyone did anything kind, etc., etc. Ego in me had also learned that this caused people to like me and think well of me. It never occurred to me that this could also sometimes cause the behavior to become tainted or manipulative.

Suddenly, the Wisdom Master started working with her office door closed. Each time I saw that closed door, I knew that somehow I had been 'false' in my behavior, but I just couldn't get 'how' or what I had done. How could courtesy to one's Wisdom Master be wrong? Maybe the door was closed for another reason, but it was my gut that was shaking, and I was pretty sure it was my behavior that had closed that door. This went on for a long time; I was miserable, never really getting the lesson and always knowing I still hadn't grasped whatever it was, even in the times when the door was open and things seemed fine.

Then, one evening when the Temple was undergoing some structural changes, as I sat at my desk, I heard the Wisdom Master walk back near my door to where the scaffolding was set up. I hesitated. Her door had been shut for several days. I <u>so</u> wanted to see her, but my ego was afraid of rejection. Trying to break through the fear, I grabbed at the old courtesy habit and called out, *"Is there something I can do to help you?"*

"No!" came the Wisdom Master's fierce reply. *"This is my Temple, and you live here by my invitation. I will walk wherever I please, whenever I please. What you said is what someone says who thinks they are being imposed upon. That was ego, not courtesy!"*

Shocked and cracked wide open at last, I suddenly realized that what she said was true.

I had blurted out those words, not from my very real love and desire to be of service to the Wisdom Master, but from my ego's fear of rejection, and my words sounded haughty. Humbled, I realized that was also what I had been doing for months: sometimes speaking and acting from true heart, and sometimes ego-performing rote behaviors of 'defensive' politeness. Often, the behaviors were the same, but their point of origin, timing, and energy were entirely different. She had always known which was which; it was I who had not.

After that, the door was almost always open.

Not Mine To Give

About a month after moving to Skycliffe, I was called into the Wisdom Master's office. When I entered the room, two other apprentices were already sitting on the floor in front of the Wisdom Master's desk. I took a seat between them.

A week earlier, I had asked my mother, who is a physician, to call in a prescription for the mother of one of the other apprentices. The apprentice's mother was visiting Skycliffe at the time and had decided to stay longer. As a result, she would be running out of some of her medicine. I had offered to ask my mom and had thought nothing of it. I was used to asking my mom for medicine for myself and my friends, and I was also accustomed to my mom's friends and family calling when they were sick and needed a prescription. My mom always seemed happy to help. But I was soon to learn that just because something is acceptable in the world doesn't mean it is right conduct.

The Wisdom Master asked how it came about that my mom had sent this medicine. The apprentice, whose mother the medicine was for, explained. Then, the Wisdom Master looked directly at me, pinning me with her eyes, and in a powerful voice that reverberated inside me said, *"Your mother is a student. It is abusing her to impose in her personal space like that, and I will not have her be abused."* I felt the uneasiness churning inside me at her words, but my eyes remained fastened on the Wisdom Master.

"When you were at school, it was different, but you represent Skycliffe now. It is not the same as at school. I am in charge here. You need to start thinking of your mom as a friend, not as someone who owes you favors."

Nodding towards the other apprentice, she said *"She could have* taken her mother to a doctor here." Then to me she added, "*I know you were just trying to be generous, but your mother's services are not yours to give.*"

She paused, looking intently at me, and then asked, "*Do you have any questions?*"

"No," I said, shaken, "*I think you were pretty clear.*"

After I left the office, the Wisdom Master's words continued to echo inside me. I started to look at my behavior towards my mom, and I began to see what the Wisdom Master was saying. I did have the attitude that what was my mom's was also mine, and I asked things of her that I wouldn't ask of anyone else. I was unconsciously taking advantage of my mom's generosity and the fact that I was her child. It was difficult to admit to myself, but once I saw it, I knew I couldn't continue acting from that mental attitude. I could see how it harmed our relationship.

When I first started to break free of this habitual energy, I would have to pause before acting and ask myself, "*Would I ask this of one of my friends?*" As I am becoming more practiced at treating my mom as an adult friend, it has become clearer how to act, and our relationship is becoming freer.

Mini-Pearl

Two dogs live at the monastery--Mini-Pearl and Dallas. Dallas will eat just about anything you give him, but Mini-Pearl is choosier. She likes the treat to be the right size and not too boring. Sometimes, she will take a treat and then set it down and look at me like she's saying, *"Can't you do better than this?"* One day it was all I had, and I told her if she didn't want it, I would give it to Dallas. She immediately ate it. I found this amusing and had an opportunity to mention it to the Wisdom Master. She said that I should not cause her to suffer like that. I didn't get it. So I asked how that caused her suffering and learned that I was encouraging Mini-Pearl to be competitive with Dallas, and that competitive behavior always causes suffering because it is not for the good of the whole.

My Father

While I knew intellectually that I was like my parents, I saw and accepted more of my mother than my father. After I moved away from home, most communication occurred through my mother. I'd phone, and if my father answered, he would quickly call for my mother. After my parents separated, I called him infrequently, and he rarely called me. While I loved my father, there was behavior I did not support.

Talking to the Wisdom Master, she looked at me and said she saw my papa in me (I was sitting in a chair across from her) and asked if he was a thoughtful person. *Thoughtful* was clarified as being a deep thinker vs. considerate. I became aware of my posture and hand positions, which were typical of my father.

After that conversation, I began to be conscious of the number of times I used those movements, and it hit me—in accepting him, I was accepting myself.

Parents

When my spouse and I moved to Skycliffe, I had difficulty dealing with the anger expressed by my parents for leaving them. They could not understand why we would move so far away. There was no way for me to explain our actions. I hoped that, in time, they would understand.

I talked to the Wisdom Master about this, and as I recall, she said that what we were doing was for the good of the whole and, in time, my parents would accept our decision. No one has the right to dictate what another person should do and how they should live their life; everyone has to live their life their own way. She also suggested that I keep in touch with my parents by calling regularly and visiting them on special occasions.

I followed the Wisdom Master's advice and found that after awhile, my mother softened her stance and accepted our decision, and the conversations became friendlier. I also discovered that my parents were able to take care of themselves quite well and by my not being so close, they became more independent. This allowed their world to expand at a time when most people's world contracts significantly.

Through the Wisdom Master, I have learned that we affect everyone around us with the energy and love that we constantly project, and that we do not need to be next door to be able to help people.

The Truth of the Matter Is...

The Wisdom Master called me into her office to discuss various items. One particular item had to do with a vacation trip she was planning. The thought was tossed around as to whether she would take apprentices on her vacation or go by herself.

At one point during this exchange of words, the conversation swayed toward the Wisdom Master's deciding to travel alone (or with one companion for the upcoming trip), and early next year taking a group of advanced apprentices to the same vacation spot. The Wisdom Master then asked that I go to her house, get her telephone book that had a little piece of paper with her travel agent's phone number, and bring it up to her office. After doing this, she wrote her agent's phone number down on a piece of paper, handed the paper to me, and asked that I telephone the agent about the change in plans.

I said, *"Okay. I have no problem telling her about the change. I can say something like, 'Wisdom Master Maticintin wants to really research the area before taking a group of apprentices. You know, she needs to do the groundwork before working with her apprentices in that region of the world."*

With that, Wisdom Master Maticintin said, *"No, I did not say that. I do not have to do any groundwork. You are twisting a story to make it work for you to communicate with him. Although the travel agent may understand such an explanation, it is not true. Don't do that."*

131

A Missed Opportunity

During a week-long visit with Wisdom Master Maticintin, she approached the subject of my spending alone time in a darkened enclosure, resembling a cave. At that time, I didn't have the foggiest notion of what she meant, but I began to expound on how I would like that, relating some experiences that I had gone through that seemed similar to me. I was inwardly very excited about the prospect of participating in her version of what I knew so much about. It was a clear case of 'open mouth, insert foot,' plus an arrogance born out of ignorance. I was totally unaware of what was happening until she smiled at me sweetly and said something to the effect of, *"Oh good, then you won't need that experience since you have already had it."*

It was a missed opportunity that still comes to mind as a marker when I catch myself trying to impress others instead of hearing them out.

Fear Release

While visiting the Wisdom Master at Between the Wind on Orcas Island, I took a walk with the Wisdom Master and two other students through the woodlands to the ocean. One of the students and I walked several steps behind her, while the third student walked beside the Wisdom Master. A snake slithered in front of me and behind the Wisdom Master. I shuddered and momentarily paused with my foot raised as the snake moved on. As we continued, another snake appeared, and I reacted the same way. This time, the Wisdom Master looked back at me but said nothing. A third snake appeared, and when I was asked what the problem was, I stated that I didn't like snakes.

During elementary school, the family dog had found a dead snake, and when I had started screaming and running away, the dog had seen it as a fun game and had run after me carrying the snake in his mouth. Even seeing a picture of a snake in a book would cause me to drop the book, and if there was a snake in a movie, I quickly covered my eyes. My seventh grade science teacher brought in a large box one day saying he had finally located a bull snake, and I was out of my seat and headed for the classroom door. As an adult, I still avoided the reptile house at zoos, sending my children in with another adult while I waited outside.

When a situation that needs addressing presents itself, I knew the Wisdom Master would take action. So I was not surprised when later in my visit she called me to join her outside the Happy House (meditation hall). I knew she had something for me, and as I approached, I was told to hold out my hands and take the snake she was holding and place it in the grass. Gulping, I held out my hands, slanting them towards the ground; the snake was placed on my palms and dropped into the grass beside the path where we were standing. I was surprised to realize the snake did not feel slimy.

Later, while working on creating a rock wall around some trees, the Wisdom Master walked past me and suggested I use a certain rock. Picking up the rock, I discovered there was a snake sleeping underneath. I put the rock back. Then, later in the same day while watering the garden, a snake slithered away to avoid the water. I started laughing because the snakes were getting progressively bigger! While pulling weeds, I sat on the grass with my feet in the dirt where I was working. Yes, you probably guessed it, a snake moved through the dirt. This time I was able to watch/observe the snake and see how easily and effortlessly it moved. When a second joined the first snake in the dirt, I rose quickly and walked away.

It was freeing to be able to observe what I saw and not get caught in the fear. After the visit, I was able to view snakes more objectively, no longer startled upon seeing them. But the story continues. After the move to Skycliffe, I sighted twenty snakes in an extended visit. One was laying in the sun, and as I walked passed, it did not move. I turned around and studied it for several minutes, noting its size, color and markings, realizing I was seeing different kinds of snakes. Upon sharing the sightings with the Wisdom Master, she commented about my being fearless.

I now have an appreciation for something I once feared, because I can see the divine that lives in the sentient life form called a snake.

"Poor Baby"

One day, I made a request of Wisdom Master Masticintin, and she responded, *"Poor baby"* and left. I stood there a bit stunned, trying to see what had happened to bring about such a response to my request. Needless to say, I was perplexed. A few days later, I bravely made my request again, and, to my dismay, received the same response. *'What's happening here?'* I thought to myself, but again, I could not see what I had done to receive that response. I waited a few more days, and when the opportunity arose, I prepared to make my request yet again. As I started to speak, I heard the echo of her words and saw that I was approaching her from a *poor-baby* stance that had the hidden agenda of *'pity me, I need this....,'* rather than simply making my request openly without hidden agenda. I saw that I habitually adopted the 'poor me' stance to manipulate situations in my favor, especially if I thought there was a possibility of being told *"No."* I approached her openly, without hidden agendas, and made the request, and it was approved.

Learning Generosity

As I was preparing for a trip to see my kids, Wisdom Master Maticintin called me in and said she had an assignment for me before I returned. Wondering what she would say, I waited for her to say more. Looking at me with a warm smile, she said, *"I want you to get $400.00 in twenty dollar bills, find an area frequented by beggars, and walk around giving away the money."* Well, the first response in my head was, *'FOUR HUNDRED DOLLARS!!! Is she nuts?'* But what I said, somewhat reluctantly, was, *"Okay, I will do it."* I left her office muttering to myself that I did not have $400 to throw away, and on and on. Finally, I decided to just let it go, go on my trip, and deal with it later.

The trip went fine, and as I was flying into Seattle on the way back, I realized that I had not done as she asked, and I knew I could not arrive without having given away the money. Fortunately, I had some time before I caught the next shuttle so I went to the ATM machine, got $400 in twenties, grabbed a cab and directed the driver to take me to an area of Seattle that would have lots of street people and beggars. He looked at me rather funny but headed out. He asked me what I was doing, and I explained my assignment, knowing he would think me nuts. He really surprised me when he said, *"What a great idea."*

We arrived in downtown near a park with many street people and beggars. I got out wondering if I would get mugged with all this money on me. Taking a deep breath, I headed out to find my first beggar. Walking up to a man sitting on the curb, I asked if he would like to have the twenty bucks I was holding in my hand. He looked up at me, then at the money, and slowly reached out to take it, saying nothing. Walking on, I looked back to find he was gone. Feeling a bit better about being amongst the beggars, I looked for my next person. I spotted a lady leaning against a building holding a shopping bag with her belongings, and as I walked up to her, she eyed me suspiciously. I could see she was tired and worn out, and her life had not been easy. I smiled at her and offered the twenty. She looked at me, then the money, and back at me. Her face transformed from old, tired, and worn to smiling with a sparkle in her eye. The smile lasted only a brief moment as she took the money and turned away. In that moment, I also transformed my entire attitude towards beggars, my own attitudes about money, and my willingness to give just for the sake of giving.

With moist eyes, and a light heart, I found my next beggar, gave him a big smile, and offered the money. He looked at me and took my hand and told me how grateful he was that someone cared enough to help him for a moment. My heart was touched deeply by his gratitude, and I began to see how very fortunate I was in my life and in the abundance I had. I also noticed the absence of my own gratitude for my abundance.

As I turned to continue, I found a crowd of beggars standing behind me, and I realized that the word was out that there was money to be had. I looked each one in the eye and said hello with a smile as I passed out the remaining money. With each person, I felt my heart opening and my own sense of gratitude growing. Finally, with the money gone, I said good-bye to them and returned to my cab for the trip to the shuttle.

Quietly I sat in the cab looking at what had happened in my experience with the beggars. I realized that I had let go of all my judgments about the beggars and their situations and now saw them as people whose karma was not very pleasant. I found myself having great compassion for their suffering and great gratitude for the abundance in my own life. I also realized that the $400 was no longer an issue, that my petty concerns about not having enough not only were unfounded, but also were preventing my experience of abundance. As we rode on, my body began to tremble and waves of energy rose up my spine in small tremors. I smiled, realizing that I had just had a most profound experience that had altered my life forever.

As a result of that experience, I began consciously noticing my attitudes about others and my tendency to judge. Setting my intention to release those behaviors, I looked for opportunities to give, either money to a beggar, my time to help others, or just having pleasant thoughts about those around me. I suddenly found it easy to follow one of the Wisdom Master's instructions to always give when asked, such as to a beggar, and do so without any judgment about what they might do with what is given. In other words, to just give for the sake of giving.

Taking Care of My Vessel

In the fall of 2004, I was at Skycliffe for an unplanned, extended six-month retreat. I was dealing with a serious illness, and the Wisdom Master had invited me to stay on beyond my planned summer visit to learn about myself and the mind-body connection that was the cause of my disease. I decided to stay.

The spiritual adventure the Wisdom Master offered me held the promise of reversing my health condition. However, it also demanded that I make radical changes. I needed to learn to let go of obsessiveness, procrastination, choices made out of convenience and letting others rule my life. Most importantly, I needed to learn to become aware of and change the unpleasant images that ran through my mind like a broken record. I was between the proverbial rock and a hard place. The potential for finally making the significant spiritual progress I desired loomed large. The Wisdom Master was offering me hope and the means to heal myself through mindfulness training versus chemotherapy and a dire-sounding prognosis.

Four months into my stay at Skycliffe, I brought my car to a mechanic to have it winterized for the 3,000-mile January drive home. A most unlikely set of circumstances followed. My car was stolen.

Emotionally, I felt victimized. And in my willingness to give away my power, I responded with comments such as *'it's just a car,'* and *'an old one at that.'* The Wisdom Master, however, would have none of that. Firmly and directly, she told me there are no coincidences. She explained that the car's being stolen was a reflection of what was going on with me and my body, which was the vehicle for my divinity. I had created a scenario to learn about the effort it takes to earn and hold a vehicle for self-realization. What I put forth to regain the car would be a sample of what it would take to regain and keep a healthy body for a long life of spiritual growth.

The days that followed were not easy ones for me. Yet they were full of energizing realizations about the power of persistence, focus, and taking personal responsibility. Throughout the period the car was missing, the Wisdom Master continually urged me to take action to get the car back. When I attempted to retreat into a false sense of separateness, the Wisdom Master made sure my actions were accompanied by plenty of companion energy. The energy she put forth in my support modeled for me and even surpassed my own efforts.

Approximately a week after the car was stolen, the phone call came. The car had been retrieved from a gravel pit two-and-a-half hours north of where it had been stolen. It appeared unharmed. I could pick it up at the lot where it had been towed. I could wait till Monday, I informed the Wisdom Master, or pay a small fee for the weekend pick-up. The Wisdom Master pantomimed a fisherman reeling in a catch. Procrastination had no part to play in this story, least of all, as we were bringing it to a close.

As a post script, the recovered car took me safely home the entire 3,000 miles. It has since made two additional round trips to Skycliffe. I am physically and mentally healthy and continuing my spiritual adventures on the path of HÜMÜH.

Learning about Joy

In order to complete the HÜMÜH coloring book, *HÜMÜHSCAPES,* everyone was invited to create or trace pictures. When Wisdom Master Maticintin asked me if I drew, my response was '*very little.*' It had been a long time since I had done any drawing, and I wondered if I could produce an acceptable picture. Tracing my first picture gave me the confidence to draw something freehand. Sketching a bird, I recalled how I had enjoyed drawing as a young child, but set it aside feeling I wasn't good enough or did not receive approval from others. With the Wisdom Master's encouragement, I am now learning about doing for the joy of doing, and not limiting myself based on other people's viewpoints.

Rushing

I was on my way to change into my robe for the 11 am meditation, and since it was nearly time to start, I was hurrying. As I passed the Wisdom Master, she stopped me, asking me why I was always rushing about. I paused, realizing that if I was hurrying, I could not be in the present moment because my attention was on worrying about being late, not where my feet were going or what was happening in the environment around me. I smiled as I saw this, thanked her, and continued on to get my robe, still quickly, but in the present moment.

It's Not What You Do...

The dining room was peaceful. The gentle clatter of typing, the rustling of paper, the hum of the computers, and the occasional murmuring from the surrounding offices created an atmosphere of quiet industry. The afternoon sun shone into the room, and the sounds of twittering birds, buzzing insects, and the bang and thump of people working outside filtered in through the screen door. But the calm did not penetrate me; I was firmly focused on the floor.

I gripped the handle of the broom, and quickly scraped the bristles across the blue tiles, picking up dirt and other errant debris. I moved hastily to get the job done, all the while, thinking of the next item on my to-do list, and wishing I could get a break from this assignment.

The screen door opened. I glanced up, and saw the Wisdom Master walk in, and another apprentice behind her. The Wisdom Master went over to one of the offices to check on the progress of an item she was waiting for. I put my head down and tried to concentrate on sweeping. Coming over and sitting at a table near where I was working, the Wisdom Master began chatting to the other apprentice and me. She watched me sweep for awhile. Then she said to me, "*You know, there was this monastery, and one of the monks had the job of sweeping the floors. Many of the other monks looked down on him. But, you know what? That monk was one of the few who became enlightened.*"

My Difficult Childhood

One time I was telling Wisdom Master Maticintin about my difficult childhood. After I had gone on and on for a while, she gave me an assignment. I was to go home and make a list of all the good things about my childhood and bring it the next day to show her.

Later, I sat down at the computer, looked at the empty screen, and thought about how short a list it was going to be, but that I had to write down *something*. And so, I began.

I remembered how we had lived near a lake, and I had the freedom to go swimming or playing on the beach whenever I liked. I remembered how we lived in the country, and I had the wonderful hills to explore. I remembered riding my horse, and learning to water-ski, and before I knew it, the good times were flowing into my mind faster than I could type. I ended up with three pages and knew that, even then, I had not gotten everything.

Eagerly, I took the list with me the next day, but the Wisdom Master never asked for it. She did not need to; doing the task was what was needed to help me see the blessings that I had been given and to put all the rest of it into perspective. Now when I think back, it isn't as if I am looking into a dark hole, but into the brightness of the opportunities that I had while growing up.

Craves Attention

The Wisdom Master used to talk with apprentices who called on the phone every Wednesday evening. On one particular Wednesday evening, she asked me to come up to her office. I was glad for the time with the Wisdom Master. Soon the phone rang. It was an apprentice who wanted to talk. I sat quietly while she conversed with the student; although, soon, I began to feel uncomfortable about listening in on this conversation. So while she was still on the phone, I excused myself. The Wisdom Master had a surprised look on her face as I got up to leave the room.

The next morning after meditation, Wisdom Master Maticintin asked if we wanted to hear a story. *"Oh, yes,"* said I, since I loved the Wisdom Master's stories. She started out telling us about someone called, *Craves Attention*. She was at least half-way through the story before I realized the story was about me and what had transpired between us the night before. She had seen me clearly once again. It was true. I craved attention from the Wisdom Master, but I wanted to be in control of that attention. She ended the story by saying that if it had been her, she would have taken every opportunity just to be near her Wisdom Master, even if she was ignored.

Worrying

In the early years of my apprenticeship with Wisdom Master Maticintin, I used to worry a lot, or so she told me. I knew I worried often, but I did not think I worried more than anyone else. It was just the way it was; I did not think too much about it until the Wisdom Master wanted me to stop worrying.

"You worry too much, and I want you to stop it," she told me.

"I worry too much? I don't think I do. Anyway, isn't it only natural to worry when there is something to worry about?" I asked.

"No, it is not natural. It is a bad habit, and if you learn not to worry, you'll be a much happier person," she said.

Yes, I would be a happier person without worrying. I could see her point, but I did not know how not to worry. To this thought she said, *"When you are worrying about something, catch yourself doing it, stop it, and then say 'No' to yourself. Say that you are not going to worry this time and put your attention away from the object or situation of your worry, put it somewhere else, on some-thing pleasant, happy, and beautiful."*

So, for the next weeks and months, I tried not to worry, to intercept worrying, to do what the Wisdom Master had told me to do. But I was not getting it. This worry thing was so deep-rooted in me that it felt like it was the under-layer of my skin. *'I must have brought this trait into this life from past lifetimes,'* I thought. *'That's why it feels like such an innate part of me.'*

The Wisdom Master kept urging me, sometimes sternly, sometimes with a mixed look in her face, and I struggled without getting anywhere. My big problem was that I did not know what 'not worrying' was like. Worrying had become so much a part of me that it felt normal and natural to me.

Then, one evening when I was sitting in a chair at home, I felt really comfortable all of a sudden, the kind of comfortable feeling that I had not experienced before. My body was relaxed, and I felt light-hearted. I said to myself, *'Ah, this must be what you feel when you don't worry,'* and remembered hearing about the Wisdom Master's lifting someone's karma temporarily to help that person.

'Oh, thank you. Now I know what it feels like not to worry. I can aim for this feeling in my body.'

I was happy. I knew now what to look for, and hoped that this feeling of not worrying would stay for a while so that I could get used to it. It lasted for a few weeks, during which time, I enjoyed the feeling of light-heartedness and ease. So when the karma was returned to me, I was in a much better position to drop this bad habit of worrying. It still took a lot of effort on my part, but it was easier, because I knew what I was doing, where I needed to go.

I also learned that I carried the 'worry energy' with me all the time whether or not I was actively worrying about something. I learned that, unless we learn to transmute this kind of energy, it is always present in us and affects our choices and decisions without us even knowing about it. That's a terrible way to live.

Much Ado about Everything

One night after the evening meditation, we remained sitting and talking with the Wisdom Master. I sensed an unusual current flow through the space and then had a sudden, very strong impulse to laugh. I tried to restrain myself because I didn't want to disturb the quiet. However, I couldn't stifle the impulse, so I covered my mouth with my hand and tried to giggle discreetly behind it. I was still trying to contain myself when I looked at the Wisdom Master and saw that the Wisdom Master had also started to laugh. Then I exploded into laughter. Although I had absolutely no idea of why I was laughing, it didn't seem to matter. Everyone there was laughing. And once we started, it seemed that we couldn't stop. I was laughing so hard that I had tears in my eyes. I laughed until my sides ached and I was doubled over. I laughed until I couldn't catch my breath and finally had to stop just to breathe. But then someone else's laugh would ignite mine, and as soon as I had breath again, I roared with laughter. The Wisdom Master was laughing as hard as everyone else. I lost all sense of time in the laughter. Finally, we stopped and ended for the night. I felt lighter after all that laughter.

The next day as I was working outside, the Wisdom Master came over and said to me that the name of last night's laugh was *much ado about nothing.* I thought it odd that a laugh would have a name. Standing next to the Wisdom Master, my perspective shifted, and I saw how I lived my life in an entirely different light. I had a moment of instant recognition. I could see how my life had been mostly *much ado about things that had no meaning.* I saw my life as an emotional roller coaster ride of highs and lows. If I got what I wanted in the moment, a new outfit at a bargain price, the job assignment I liked, a nice vacation, I was up/happy. But when I got things I didn't want, I was down/angry. In that moment, I could see that I was always at the effect of how I felt, and even more importantly, I could see that none of these things were really important. That was why I had laughed. The Wisdom Master had shown me how absorbed I was in things that had no purpose. It is always much better to laugh, and laugh, and laugh. It opened up space for me to see that what is really important in life is to be spiritually happy.

Winking Out

"Don't you dare bat your eyes!" the Wisdom Master said. I was sitting in her office, and she had just told me that I was arrogant.

This was not the first time she had spoken to me about being arrogant or batting my eyes. Years before, when I had visited her on Orcas Island, she had stopped during a Teaching and said to me, "*You need to become conscious of how often, and when, you blink. You need to learn not to flutter your eyes when I'm speaking to you. When you do, you mentally leave the room and are not present for that split second.*" At another moment during that visit, she had said, "*You know, you have a subtle way of being quite arrogant. I want you to accept that and look for how it expresses itself so you can drop it.*"

I had been deeply shocked by both statements. '*My goodness,*' I thought '*a person has to blink to protect their eyes, don't they? And isn't arrogance bragging and showing off that you have more or think you're better than someone else? Why, I don't do that.*' Or, did I? I thought about it for months afterward. I did catch times when the tone of my voice implied superior knowledge of something. I tried to correct that. But the blinking thing I didn't get at all. I had sensitive eyes; that was all.

Now, here I was in the Wisdom Master's office years later. Through her patient, persistent love, I had grown some in trust and openness, and I knew the Wisdom Master had to be right. I looked up at her with my eyes wide open, and as I gazed firmly into her eyes, I felt the urge to blink...to disappear, to 'wink out' of this uncomfortable moment, to hide, not from her, but from the knowledge of my ego's subtle duplicity and cleverness. I realized that I wanted to 'look' like I was in complete surrender and yet find a way to hide a little piece of myself...so I batted my eyes, a secret escape and a subtle, wordless protest of my innocence. How arrogant!

I was horrified as I took it in and accepted it at last, but then, a huge sense of wonder and relief flooded through me. As I continued to gaze steadfastly into the Wisdom Master's eyes, the urge to blink dissolved, my heart opened wide, and laughter welled up inside.

How blind and foolish I had been! She had 'Seen' me all along. It was only I who hadn't seen myself.

A Wise Person

One morning there was a magical happening at Skycliffe. After
HÜMing and taking a walk to the pond, there was a feeling of being
One with everything around us. There was motion around us, and,
at the same time, stillness. Maybe it was the stillness of our minds.
I don't know, because it doesn't make sense to say there is motion
and stillness at the same time.

Anyway, the Wisdom Master asked me to write about the
experience. I said I would and proceeded up to my room. While the
computer was starting up, I turned to a page at random in *A
Hundred Thousand Songs of Milarepa* and started to read. I did not
know it at the time, but this became a distraction, as well as
dissipating the energy. As I was setting the parameters on my
computer to write the story, I was preoccupied by the song I had
just read. All of a sudden, my mind became filled with chatter.

I thought it best to do another project and then get back to the
story later, when my mind was quieter. As I began on the project,
which was a pretty intense typesetting job, I decided to take a break
and call a friend. We were on the telephone about 45 to 50 minutes.
Again, I was dissipating energy.

Then, I decided to play music, still another distraction. While I
was listening to the music, Wisdom Master Maticintin asked to see
me. As I entered her office, she asked, *"How are you doing with the
story?"*

"I haven't gotten to it yet," I told her. *"I was working on the
typesetting job,"* I added, handing it to her.

She asked, *"What else did you do this morning?"*

"I spoke to a friend on the telephone," I told her.

She stood right in front of me and said, *"You lost it! You dissipated the experience."*

As she repeated the word *'dissipate,'* she sort of melted to the floor. Yes, it had been like *'melting* to the floor.' The lesson of dissipating the energy of the story and the accompanying picture of her melting to the floor really stuck in my mind.

I assured the Wisdom Master that the next time she asked me to write a happening here at Skycliffe, I will STOP everything I am doing and write.

Shortly thereafter, I presented a writing to the Wisdom Master about the above experience. She did not like what I wrote saying, *"I want the story that goes with the energy, not just the energy only. The story is the parallax."* After I digested her words, she added, *"It is not a wise person who throws the gift of power away."*

The Beggar's Gift

I had come back to California after an extended stay at Skycliffe. I felt like a fish out of water. I was on a personal mission to clean up some karma that was weighing me down and holding me back. There was a pervasive feeling of depression because I didn't know quite where to start. Having moved to a new town, I was not only unfamiliar with the surroundings, I was also unused to the hustle and bustle of city life—the noise, the crowds, and the hurry.

I had driven to town in my car to find window shades for my new cottage. As I came up to a light where I was to make a U-turn, the light turned red. There, on the cement island, was a beggar, swaying in the wind. He was unwashed, disheveled, wearing dirty clothes. He held a sign that said, *"Hungry. Please help."* I could hear Wisdom Master Maticintin's voice in my head, *"Don't pass a beggar. Give half of whatever you have."*

Looking away, I fumbled for my purse. As I opened my wallet, I saw a couple of one's and a ten dollar bill. In all honesty, I must say I hesitated, speaking to my own mind, *'You've only just moved here; you don't have much money to set up house. Maybe you should give him the one's.'* But at the same time, two dollars was only one-fifth of what I had, and it felt wrong for me to keep ten and give only two. Instantly, a higher consciousness kicked in, *'Oh, for heaven's sake, trust.'* I quickly pulled out the ten and handed it through the window to him. It took a moment to get his attention. Perhaps when I turned away to search through my purse, he had thought I was avoiding him. As he took the money, it was a moment before he registered that it was a ten dollar bill, not a one dollar bill.

Then his eyes brightened, and a wide smile broke out on his

154

face revealing missing teeth, and he exclaimed, *"Whoa. No way!"* He laughed and looked into my eyes. Then he held up two fingers in a peace sign. I reflected his peace sign by holding up my fingers.

Then he did the unexpected. Very slowly, he reached with his two fingers toward my two fingers. Again, I hesitated, *'Do I want this man to touch me?'* And again, instantly came back, *"Oh, for goodness sake!"* And our two peace signs touched. I recall how smooth and silky his fingers were.

Then the light turned green. I released my foot from the brake and made the intended U-turn.

What a gift that beggar had given! I was transformed from uncertainty, fear, depression, and self-pity to a state of jubilation, upliftment, and a feeling of oneness with life. All at once, I was at home in this bustling, noisy, busy city. I can only hope he received as much as I did that day.

A phrase from the *Invocation for a Happy Life* comes to me now: *"To be at one with the gift given or received."*

Same Old; Same Old

One afternoon, coming out of the dining room, I saw Wisdom Master Maticintin sitting on the porch reading some papers. I moved quietly past her, stepping off the porch and heading out to the Stupa. As I walked away, the Wisdom Master called out to me, *"Anything new?"* I stopped and turned around. Looking at her, I pursed my lips in thought for a second, and then with a slight shrug and a shake of my head, casually said, *"No,"* thinking to myself, *'I am doing the same jobs I have been doing for the past couple of weeks. Same old; same old.'*

She looked intently at me and, with an astonished note in her voice, said, *"Nothing's new?"* I furrowed my brow, knowing I was missing something. Then my eyes went wide with the thought, *'Oh, a new day...a new moment. Am I living a moment free of my habitual energy?'* Well, obviously not. I grinned, laughing at myself.

The Egg

I was walking to the dining room, but my mind was on other things. The Wisdom Master happened to see me and said, *"Where are you?"* I was puzzled. Then she had me alternately pat my head and stamp my foot. She seemed satisfied with the results of that, but later, when she saw me again, she handed me a raw egg. I was to carry it with me wherever I went to help me stay in the present moment. Surprisingly, I was able to forget that I had it with me, and I nearly dropped it a few times. That quickly brought me back into the present moment. Four days later, I carefully disposed of it after telling the Wisdom Master that the egg's energy was beginning to feel bad. She looked at me and asked why I would carry around something that felt bad. Two lessons from one egg!

Lost Cat

For years, I had a beautiful white and grey cat named Bella, whom I loved. When I was planning to come to Skycliffe for a three-month retreat, I was concerned about what I should do with her during that time. My friends, who lived in the country had graciously offered to take her. However, I had lived with my cat there before, and Bella had turned out to be very scared of the outdoors and subsequently decided she wouldn't go outside anymore. I had lived the past two years in a city apartment, and she hadn't been outside, other than hanging out on the balcony. She seemed to live a contented life. Now, I was all worried about disrupting her life and getting her used to a new place again and the long car ride to get there.

I had the idea to take her for a short ride in the car every day and then take her 'for a walk' in the outdoors with a halter, so that she could get used to being outside again. On the first day of our outing, I had taken her to a nearby park with old-growth forest; she was scared and didn't move much. On the second day, she started walking quickly, and I thought I would let her lead me. When she wanted to duck into the underbrush, I gently pulled her back, but she slipped right through the halter and disappeared into the underbrush.

My first reaction was calmness – I thought she would come out soon. So I sat and chanted the Mantra. But no Bella showed up. I called her, looked for her, but she was nowhere to be seen. I went home and got some food and water and a shirt of mine to leave there for her in case she showed up when I was not there. I went back to the forest for hours at a time, calling her, looking for her, sitting in meditation, chanting the Mantra, but I never saw her again. I posted posters with her picture in the neighborhood, called local animal shelters

158

– all to no avail.

When I came to Skycliffe, I asked to speak to the Wisdom Master, and I brought up the issue of my lost cat. The Wisdom Master told me a story, which I remember as such: *"Once, a long time ago, there was a monk who went to live in a monastery with Sakyamuni. Now, this monk had a golden elephant, which was beautiful. Sakyamuni said to the monk that he could not bring the elephant with him. He would attract too much attention, and the beast, while gentle, would be too much of a distraction. That evening, the monk went to the elephant and told him that he was going to live in a monastery and that he couldn't bring him. The following night, the elephant died in his sleep."*

At the time when Wisdom Master Maticintin told me the story, I didn't really understand it. I remember thinking: *'But I'm not moving to a monastery – I was just going for three months.'* Little did I know, that I was going to extend my three-month retreat to become a long-term resident. I knew there was an implication of responsibility that things had turned out with Bella as they did, but I wasn't quite sure how.

When I started looking closer at the issue, I began to see that I might have set up the situation – unconsciously – to lose her. When I brought it up during a private conversation with the Wisdom Master, she said: *"Yes, you took her to the forest and let her loose."* That really hit me. Although I felt strongly that it wasn't my intention to do so, I remembered that first feeling of calmness – no true concern, when she didn't come out. Then, of course, I felt guilty and did what I thought I should and wanted to do to find her. This was all very difficult to admit to myself.

Reflecting back, I knew that I had been struggling with cat allergies and asthma for years. Although I had difficulties breathing, I had this strong conviction that I would never give up my cats because of allergies. I was very opinionated and judgmental about people who did 'that kind of thing' because of their own inconvenience. I could also see that I was often impatient with Bella's neediness, which, I understand now, truly just mirrored my own neediness. I could see that my thoughts and mental images were that of a flip-flop of love and resentment.

The day when I talked to the Wisdom Master about my cat, she also told me that Bella was fine and happy, and that she was with a man. Hearing this brought all the relief to my aching heart that I could ask for. Now I knew that she was happy and in a safe place, and I vowed to become more aware of my mental images, thoughts, and actions so that I would not harm any more sentient beings.

The Wisdom Master suggested that I consciously give service in Bella's name. Since I was gathering rocks at that time for a path we were building, she told me to pick up each rock, praying to the divine consciousness for Bella's happiness and well-being, which I did. I did not completely understand why at the time, but I could feel a burden being lifted. It was an opportunity to transmute the negative karma that I had created through my thoughts and actions. It stopped the cycle of dwelling in those feelings and ultimately creating similar experiences. I was able to forgive myself and subsequently felt lighter and a little bit happier for both of us.

There Are No Accidents

A Daily Wisdom Teaching sent by the Wisdom Master to students stated the following:

"Accidents are a product of one's lack of attention to the moment and, very often, the attention is focused on something negative." Shaman of Tibet pg 286

This reminded me of a letter I wrote to the Wisdom Master several years ago about a car accident that I had been involved in. I had carefully outlined the details of the accident and explained how the other driver was legally at fault. I received the following response from the Wisdom Master:

"Accidents are terrible things, because they send the mind into a tailspin trying to figure out what happened. The important thing now is gratitude and acceptance that you were given divine assistance. Also, it is important to realize that when our attention is split, we draw problems or accidents to ourselves. Such a realization is not to berate ourselves after the fact, but to become more focused in the present moment."

This lesson about how we are responsible for EVERYTHING that happens to us and the need for becoming more focused on the present moment has taken a while for me to truly comprehend. I am very grateful for this Teaching. It has made me a safer driver and increased my awareness about taking responsibility for ALL my actions.

The Stupa Pond

The rocks that surrounded the newly created, small pond at the back of the Stupa would not remain in place; they kept sliding into the water. I was asked to position some wooden stakes in order to provide support. Two stakes were easily placed, but the third required the use of a hammer to slide it under the rocks. Sensing I had made an error, I withdrew the stake and saw a slit in the pond lining. Reinserting the stake in another manner, I tucked that error into a corner of my mind.

When the pond started loosing water, Wisdom Master Maticintin asked if I knew what the problem was. I denied being the cause of the problem, while the Wisdom Master observed the pond.

A few days later, while meditating, the error I had made popped out of that tucked away mental place. Oh, no, now I needed to face the truth and correct the situation. What would the Wisdom Master say or do? Finding Wisdom Master Maticintin, I explained what I'd done. Her response surprised me. I was told what to do in order to correct the problem. There were no fierce looks, no disapproval, only guidance.

Later, the Wisdom Master explained to me that by being honest and setting aside vanity, I became trustworthy.

Two Halves

One day as I was leaving the Wisdom Master's office, I said, *"Is there anything I can get you?"*

Looking up from writing, the Wisdom Master replied, *"It's what you withhold that holds you back."*

Stunned by her reply, I stood immobilized, silently letting the words sink in. She looked down and continued writing. Finally, I said, *"Thank you,"* bowed, and left. I had just been given a clue—one that never would have occurred to me.

After that, I began to notice when a sense of inner 'withholding' was suddenly present, even when outwardly I was doing what was needed or what had been asked. I discovered that if I could catch that feeling and then let the source of my action drop deeper, past the habitual self, and into the heart of the Divine Consciousness within me, the sense of withholding would dissolve into a joyous upwelling of energy to accomplish whatever I had set out to do.

Several weeks later, I said to the Wisdom Master, *"Thank you for pointing out that it is what I withhold that holds me back. I've been seeing some of 'how' and 'when' I do that."*

Before I could say any more, she smiled and said, *"And it is also the generosity of what you give that moves you forward."*

163

A Meeting with the Wisdom Master

Several years ago, I was very worried about money, so the Wisdom Master gave me a series of assignments.

She told me, *"I want you to seek out beggars and give money to them. For your first assignment, look for one beggar per day and give him or her $20. Do this every day for one week."*

At that time in my life, $20 seemed rather a great deal of money to give to just one beggar, but I decided that I would do what she asked me to do. So with a $20 bill in my pocket for easy reach, I headed for London Drugs on Broadway in Vancouver. I knew that there were at least four or five beggars at any given moment, every day, in front of that store; and I even knew their faces. I also decided to give the money to the first beggar I saw in front of the store.

When I got to the store, however, I was surprised that there were no beggars, except for this new beggar with black unruly hair, one eye, and distorted lips in a dark, reddened face, standing at the entrance to the store. Quietly I said to myself, *'Oh, no, not him. He is very ugly.'* I did not want to give the money to him. Instead of giving the money to the first beggar I saw, I quickly decided that I was going into the store, buy something, and if he was still there when I came out, then I would give the money to him. If he wasn't, well, too bad, the money would have to go to someone else.

While in the store, my conscience bothered me. I asked myself, *'What difference does it make if the beggar is 'ugly?' Am I stupid enough to allow appearance to dictate my actions?'* I had thought I had risen above that type of prejudice, but clearly, I had not. My reactions to this man's appearance pointed to my own short-comings and I felt ashamed. By the time I was paying at the cashier, I was praying that he would still be there.

Grabbing my bag of purchases from the counter, I dashed out of the door, and to my relief, he was still there. I curbed my enthusiasm just then and paused to make sure that I was in the state of extended awareness. The Wisdom Master had instructed me, *"Be sure you are focused at the Third Eye when you give the money to the beggar. Do not have any expectations or make any mental comments."*

When I felt that I was in Third Eye Vision, I approached the man and handed him the $20. His whole face broke into a great, beautiful smile when he said, *"Thank you,"* and I swear there was a twinkle in his good eye. I could not believe that such a deformed face could be so beautiful. I felt deeply moved and tears started to stream down my cheeks.

Embarrassed at my own response to the experience, I smiled, backed up quickly, and turned around and left. I cried all the way to the office where I worked. As I write this story today, it still has the same effect on me.

That evening I e-mailed the Wisdom Master with the details of the experience. The following morning she responded by saying, simply, *"Thank you for the $20."*

Buried Alive

One day as I was working on a project, Wisdom Master Maticintin came to me and said, *"Carry this piece of plywood and come with me."* I grabbed the plywood and hurried after her as she took off down a lane into the woods. After a brief walk, we came to a place, and she said to dig a hole in the earth large enough for me to lie down. I could sense this urgency about her directions and began quickly trying to dig the hole. The earth was filled with brush and roots of the forest, and I dug and pushed, wishing all the while that she would slow down and stop pushing me so hard to hurry up. Then the Wisdom Master said, *"Okay, that is enough. Now, lie down in the hole."* I lay in the hole on my back, pulling the plywood sheet over me, and she began covering me with forest debris and dirt. As I lay there, I could see the daylight fading with the nightfall and with the covering of the hole. I had the thought, *'Oh, boy, this is going to be fun.'*

Well, night fell, darkness arrived, and so did the bugs and the dampness of the earth and the night. I lay there with my mind going 90 miles an hour, busily chattering about my discomfort and wondering what magical experience I was to have during the night. After awhile, I fell asleep.

During the night, I had a dream, and in the dream I crawled out of the hole and went off wandering into town. During my wandering, I accumulated quite a large sum of money. Upon returning to the hole, I passed the Wisdom Master and other students, one of whom was my wife, busily working in the forest. As I passed by, I gave the money to my wife to hold for me until the next day.

My next awareness was hearing the Wisdom Master's voice calling me to awaken. She cleared the debris and dirt from the plywood,

166

and I emerged into the morning. She told me to go get cleaned up and have breakfast, and we would talk about the night.

Later, as we met for meditation and talk, I shared the story of the dream with her. She immediately, rather strongly, pointed out that I had completely missed the opportunity of the experience by leaving and going in search of money; and then, by giving the money to my wife, I had also impaired my wife's experience of being with her Wisdom Master.

As I had begun to share my dream, I was quite excited about it since I rarely remember my dreams. Hearing the Wisdom Master so clearly tell me that I had blown the entire experience, I was devastated and felt foolish.

As I looked at that experience to see what lessons there were for me, I began to see some of my habitual patterns of life. Probably the biggest was my need for comfort and my hidden agenda of wanting things my way, but all the while professing that I was not that way. The Wisdom Master often called me "The Great Pretender" in those days. The feelings of being rushed and wanting more time to get the hole more comfortable both reflected those patterns. Writing this story some years later, I now realize that while I gave some thought to what I saw, I was still unwilling, at the time, to change. Slowly over the time since then, I have become more and more aware of my pretenses and habitual behavior. It is always an ever-ongoing challenge for me to stay present enough to see them.

Contemplation

In the kitchen one morning, the Wisdom Master walked up to me and told me that I was 'mischievous.' *"Surely, you must know this about yourself by this time,"* she added.

As she walked out the door, I called out, *"Is that good or bad?"*

"Neither," she replied with a smile.

Then, she left.

The Rock

When I moved to Skycliffe to become a resident, I was 26-years-old, and I had never had a real job. All I had done was go to school, and occasionally, when the whim had struck me, I had gotten a part time job, but never anything I had taken too seriously. I didn't really need the job; my mom provided everything I needed, and more.

In many ways, even though I was 26-years-old, I was still playing the role of the child. But I wasn't happy with that arrangement anymore. I wanted to be independent of my mom. I wanted to start taking responsibility for myself and have the freedom that came from that. Being at Skycliffe with the Wisdom Master's support and encouragement was giving me the opportunity to do that. During those first few months, I did start to take responsibility for the more mundane aspects of my life; however, I still had a lot to learn about self-discipline and taking responsibility for my own spiritual evolvement.

The Wisdom Master was working at her computer as I entered her office and sat down on the purple cushion, angling myself to face her desk. She stopped and looked over at me, asking, *"Have you been moody?"*

Warning bells went off. I said, *"Well, I've been thinking about my attention."*

"Do you think you had your attention with me yesterday?" she asked, a firmness in her voice.

Shaking my head and looking down at my hands, I replied, *"No, not at all. I was looking in at myself."* Images from the previous morning flashed through my mind. The Wisdom Master and another apprentice had been standing on the path talking, and I had walked past, keeping my head down and not making eye contact, thinking to

169

myself, *'Don't notice me.'* As I came even with them, the Wisdom Master, smiling, had called out, *"Hi."* I had glanced up, given a perfunctory greeting, then had quickly put my head back down and scurried away. When I had gotten a little ways down the path, I had suddenly stopped and said, *"Oh, my gosh, what did I just do? That was incredibly rude."* My stomach had felt a bit queasy. I had taken a deep breath and said to myself, *'Well, I can't go back and change it. I will just have to be more aware of doing that—trying not to see anyone so that I don't feel I have to acknowledge them, even the Wisdom Master.'* Then I had gone on with my day, but I had not been surprised when I had been called into her office that morning.

I glanced up at the Wisdom Master and saw her purse her lips together and start going, *"Mmhhhmmm...mmmhhmmm,"* as she swiveled her chair this way and that, looking around her desk area. At first I thought she was making a show of ignoring me, like I ignored her the previous day. But then, as she continued to scrutinize her work area, turning away from me to look at the window ledge behind her desk, I realized she was looking for something. She picked something up from the window ledge and turned back around to face me. She started to reach her hand towards me, so I rose to my knees and moved closer to the front of her desk, reaching out my right hand. She placed a grey heart-shaped rock in my hand. It had some heft to it; it was about four inches wide.

Looking directly into my eyes, she said, *"You are not to take this rock out of your hand until I say otherwise. Have it when you shower, when you go to the bathroom...hopefully, this will teach you to be mindful."*

My eyes went a little wide and my mind started saying, *'But I am right-handed...* (The hand in which she had placed the rock)' However, I didn't say anything. I took a deep breath, and thought to myself, *'Well, this should be interesting. I guess I am going to learn how to use my left hand.'*

She stated, *"You are one-handed,"* and with that, she turned back to her computer and resumed typing, a clear dismissal. I rose slowly, rock in hand, bowed, and backed out of the room.

After leaving the Wisdom Master's office, I headed out to the stable. It was one of the mornings I helped with picking up manure. At first, it was awkward trying to use the rack with only my left hand, but eventually I figured out a workable system, though I still had to be very aware of what I was doing. Later, at lunch, as I tried to eat with one uncoordinated hand, I got another lesson in being mindful of the simple things. Part of me found the whole thing amusing, and another part was trying to figure out what I was supposed to be learning so I could get rid of the rock.

Later that afternoon, the Wisdom Master called me into her office again. Without preamble, she said, *"I don't feel comfortable taking you anymore,"* referring to a trip she had asked me to accompany her on. I nodded my head in understanding, not surprised; the rock in my hand a heavy and blatant reminder of my inability to control my mind. She then said, *"I am going to ask someone else to come."* I nodded my head again, looking down at my rock-filled hand. I could see why the Wisdom Master couldn't take me, but I still felt a moment of disappointment.

She paused and then asked, *"Is it helping?"*

"Yes," I said, looking back up at the Wisdom Master. *"I can feel it in my hand, and it reminds me what I am supposed to be doing – being mindful."* With some exasperation, I confessed, *"I feel my mind is out of control. I think I have the attention of a two-year-old...maybe less."*

She smiled at me, saying, *"Maybe not a two-year-old, but an eighteen-year-old."* Then, she continued, *"You follow your best friend's energy* (referring to a friend that lived at a distance who I was concerned did not approve of the life-style I had chosen). *It is like you are on a leash. Is she an honorable person?"*

I hesitated.

"You know, it might be three years, and you will still be carrying that rock. You are going to have calluses on your hand," she stated.

I just stared at my rock with an expression of 'what have I gotten my self into' and let out a big sigh, looking at an inscrutable puzzle.

The Wisdom Master let out a hearty laugh.

"But I have to get this," I said with conviction, furrowing my brow.

"Yes," she replied. Then smiling at me, she said *"You could tape it to your hand to give your hand a rest."*

"There is an idea," I said, grinning at her.

"You're lucky I didn't give you a boulder." I smiled. Then, we both stood up, and she walked me out the door saying, *"Hopefully, you will get to go with me some other time."*

By that evening, the novelty of the rock was starting to wear off. I wanted to stretch out my fingers, which were hot and sweaty, having been heated by my body. The urge to let go of the rock rose in me, but the Wisdom Master said it was not to leave my hand, so I tried to put my attention on something else and allow the feeling to pass. Later that night, I took a shower, rock in hand, clumsily trying to keep the soap from slipping away from me as I tried to figure out how to wash my left arm. The absurdity of the situation hit me, and I started to laugh. What a predicament I had created for myself.

Before I went to bed, I read some of the earlier discourses on mindfulness, attempting to gain some clarity. I started to see how I had become obsessive about developing a quiet mind. I had been driven, constantly staring at how important mindfulness was, until I started to become fearful I wouldn't be able to do it, which, of course, was not the way to develop a quiet mind, quite the opposite. So, by the time I walked past the Wisdom Master, I was completely turned inward. I also looked at the phrase from the Bodhisattva Prayer: "*...to be mind-ful of body...feelings,...mind, and mental objects...Such mindfulness, born of inner silence,...forges the road to power...that brings about concentration, which, in turn, brings about joyful perseverance with mental imagery that is inquisitive, daring, or bold...*" I knew I was still back at the "*mindfulness, born of inner silence*" part. I needed to cultivate inner silence so that I could begin to develop mindfulness. As I sat there looking at those words, it occurred to me that a part of doing that was giving up distractions, anything that took my attention away from my spirituality, from the inner quiet. I had been wondering for awhile if I should give up movies and books, other than the Wisdom Master's, until I was more adept at mindfulness. They just seemed to draw me in and stir up desire. Putting all those images in my mind wasn't going to help cultivate inner silence, so I resolved that, for now, I would give them up.

Finally, I decided to call it a night. I got out an ace bandage and snuggly wrapped the rock in my hand. I only slept four hours before I woke up. My wrist was sore from the unaccustomed weight of the rock, so I rotated my wrist, trying to stretch out the tendons and muscles. Eventually, I found a position that relieved some of the weight from my wrist. After awhile, my mind settled down, and I fell back asleep.

The next morning was an assigned day of rest for me. An hour before the morning meditation, I got some tea from the kitchen and sat out on the porch. I watched the birds and chipmunks and practiced just being. There was a tranquility and beauty to the morning; spring just beginning to get into full swing. I could feel this inner calm forming in me. I gave myself to it, no thoughts, just an awareness of it, of the feeling of it in my body. There was a lightness and quiet joy. When I felt it start to slip, I would just relax, and it would become balanced again. I was curious about this feeling, and so I concentrated on maintaining it. I went to the morning meditation in that space and had the best meditation I had ever had.

I spent the rest of the day hiking in the woods and sitting by the river. It was the first sunny and warm day of the year. As I was walking and climbing up hills, I was aware of the rock in my hand, and I made adjustments because I knew I couldn't use that hand to catch myself, but I wasn't focusing on it. I was aware of my surroundings. I lay in the grass watching the ants industriously explore the ground and the birds fly overhead and into nearby trees. I practiced standing on one foot on logs, and jumping back and forth, finding that balance point. I listened to my surroundings, surprised at all the sounds I had never heard. There was an aliveness and brightness to everything. I was surrounding myself with quiet to nurture the silence I had begun to discover within me.

After that day, I started to take more walks and spend time just being by myself in nature, sitting by the river and learning about impermanence. When I went for walks, I would go in whatever direction felt right without a lot of mental chatter, taking paths that presented themselves and exploring areas of the property I hadn't seen. This had always been something I wanted to do, but I had been so caught up in my habitual energy, I had never done it.

However, in the first week, I was new at this and still slipped up. Even after the wonderful experiences I had, there was still resistance in me. Sometimes it felt like the rock was a weapon. There was all this energy in my arm and hand. I could feel the resistance rise up in me, usually as an urge to throw the rock away or as an image of throwing the rock at something. At first, I was shocked and startled by this surge of violent energy, but I knew getting caught up in guilt about it was not the way to release it. So, I laughed. I laughed a lot, shaking my head and saying to myself, *'Here we go again.'* Then, I would shift my attention. Sometimes I would have to do it over and over again, but I just kept at it. I thought about how the Wisdom Master said it took five seconds before a karmic cycle got started, so I didn't let myself focus on the images longer than that, and I hoped that I wasn't harming anyone.

Also during this initial time of resistance, I felt useless because I couldn't do all the things I usually did. I knew that came from being focused on self, but I couldn't always shake the feeling. One afternoon in particular, it started to really bother me. I had been asked to replace the old green tarps on the garden shed with new ones. The old ones had to be taken off and the new ones had to be cut to size and stapled on with a staple gun. I asked another apprentice to help me because I knew my left hand wasn't strong enough by itself to use the staple gun. However, I wasn't very coordinated with the scissors either, so the other apprentice ended up doing most of the work, and I offered what assistance I could, which basically entailed holding the end of the tape measure and holding the tarp in place when she stapled it to the garden shed beams. I felt bad about this, and towards the end, I became frustrated with the situation. I insisted on trying to hammer in some of the staples that hadn't gone in all the way, even if it took me forever with my left hand.

After we were done, I was exhausted. I went to my room and lay down. It occurred to me while I was lying in bed that I was tired because of all the resistance I had created towards my rock that afternoon. So, I stopped focusing on my rock, and started watching a couple of spiders crawling on the ceiling. Before I knew it, I wasn't tired anymore.

Over the next few days, I began to learn to use my left hand. I had to do many things backwards from how I would normally have done them. Simple things, like cutting a piece of cheese or where I placed the dust pan when I swept. As a result, I began to become more aware of how I had been operating from unconscious habitual energy, especially with the more mundane daily tasks. Using my left hand was forcing me to stay mindfully awake.

However, my mind was still trying to figure out what I needed to do to let the rock go: *What was I supposed to be learning? What did I need to realize to get rid of the thing?* And as I started to become more aware of some of my habitual behavior, the questions turned to: *Am I getting what I am supposed to? Am I missing something?* I knew that such mental chatter wouldn't bear any fruit, but the thoughts seemed to come unbidden. All I could do was turn my attention away when they arose, and not allow myself to obsess.

On Saturday morning, I walked with the Wisdom Master to her car; she was leaving on her trip with the two other apprentices.

"How are you doing? Been moody?" she asked

"I realize I have been obsessing." I answered.

"You know, if you do that to yourself, you do it to others," she said, peering over at me.

I didn't say anything. A part of me understood that it was the same principle as if you are self-critical, you are critical of others, but I wasn't sure how obsession fit into that axiom. Did she mean I obsessed about other people? She smiled at me as if she understood I didn't completely get it; we walked in silence for a few moments. Then, I started to mention some of the things I had been learning.

As we continued to talk, I could feel a part of me still wishing I could go with the Wisdom Master and trying not to kick myself for losing the opportunity. The Wisdom Master turned and looked intently at me for a moment. Then, she said, *"Would you do something for me while I am gone?"*

"Sure," I said enthusiastically.

"Use your upliftment to uplift others," she said.

"Okay, I can do that," I replied.

She smiled.

I bowed and said, *"Have a good trip."* Then, I turned and walked back towards the Padma Valley gate. As I opened the gate, I thought of what the Wisdom Master had asked me to do. I knew that there wasn't anything really to do; all I had to do was just *be*, continuing to nurture the silence I had found on Wednesday. That was what would be uplifting to the whole.

That evening, I received an e-mail from another apprentice. She had sent me a Wisdom Teaching from two years ago. It stated: *"...Be as you wish to be. Function in the most natural way. When you feel yourself relaxed and comfortable both within and without, then you will know you are serving the Divine Force."* It was exactly what the Wisdom Master had asked me to do. I took it to heart. Anytime I started to get anxious or frustrated, I would tell myself to just be, to relax. I continued to listen to the Teachings on mindfulness, habitual energy, and developing a quiet mind. On my day off, I still went to the meditations in the Temple because it helped me to concentrate better. I got too distracted at home. I remembered the Wisdom Master's saying that what you put your attention on is what you manifest in your life. So, I practiced keeping my attention on my spirituality, on developing a quiet mind. I also began to see how my need for my best friend's approval stemmed from my attachment to our relationship, and how that attachment stifled our relationship. I decided to let go, follow my heart, and allow her to do the same; to hold the friendship in the open palm of my hand.

At lunch the day after the Wisdom Master returned from her trip, she called down from the head of the table to me, *"How is Rocky?"*

I grinned and said, *"Great."*

She looked intently at me and said, *"You look different."* Then, grinning, she jokingly added, *"You are going to be carrying that rock until you have a beard."* Everyone laughed.

The following day, I had an appointment with a chiropractor who came up from Vancouver to Skycliffe every few months. The morning of my appointment, I started thinking about how my rock might cause some difficulty with certain adjustments. By the afternoon, I was debating whether or not it would be okay to put down the rock just for the fifteen-minute appointment. It would make things easier.

But the Wisdom Master had said I couldn't put the rock down unless she said otherwise, so I decided to ask her. I was trying not to be attached to the outcome, but I was a little nervous about asking her. I had never gone over to her office without being called there. When the afternoon meditation was over, I went to her office door, which was open, and knocked. She looked up from her work, smiled at me, and said, *"Come in,"* leaning back in her chair. As I walked into her office, she said, *"Let me see your hand. I don't want you to be tearing it up."* I walked up to her desk and moved the rock, without letting it go, so that she could inspect my hand. She looked at my hand, which was fine, and said, *"You have been taking care of yourself."*

"Yes," I answered. *"There is this one spot here,"* I said, pointing to the upper left corner of my palm, *"The rock rubs against there at night, but I put some moleskin over the area so I don't get a blister."*

She chuckled.

Then, lowering my eyes and shifting my feet, I asked, *"Can I put the rock down while I am at the chiropractor?"*

"No." I looked up at her response. *"That's life,"* she said firmly, but kindly.

"That's life, huh?" I said, echoing her, and tilting my head to the side. *"Okay."*

She looked penetratingly at me and then said, *"The idea is to be in the present moment where there is no thought of self."* Then, in answer to my unspoken questions, she said, *"If you don't put attention on it, neither will he. If he asks about it, say you have an attachment."* She grinned, and my face creased into a smile. Then, she continued, *"And if he asks if you can take it out, say, 'No, thank you. I have an assignment and I am going to follow through'."*

"Okay, thank you." I said smiling at her. I felt uplifted. I realized that I was glad she had said no. So many times in my life, I had found reasons, of course all valid, why I couldn't follow through with something I had set out to do. This time, with the Wisdom Master's sup-

port, I was going to make the impeccable choice. I went to the chiropractor with my rock in hand. He did ask about it, but I followed the Wisdom Master's advice, and all went well.

Later, remembering the conversation with the Wisdom Master, I was struck by what she had said—that being in the present moment meant no thought of self. I started to see all the little ways I was focused on myself. I realized that the mental chatter going through my mind was all self-centered. So, I began to be vigilant about catching the mind chatter. At first, I would catch myself after the fact, then midway through a thought, and eventually, I began to develop an awareness of how my body would tense up just before the mind chatter started. It all went back to relaxing and allowing myself to be. At that point, I just gave in. I let go of trying to figure out what I was supposed to be learning or wondering when it would be over, and just started to live in the present moment.

Several mornings later, I was walking up the little hill from the kitchen when I heard the Wisdom Master call my name. I looked in the direction of her voice; she was standing on the Temple steps. I quickly went over to her.

She asked, *"How are you doing?"*

"Good," I answered.

Looking down at my rock, she said, *"Your rock is getting very smooth. It is becoming a friend; one that doesn't talk back."*

I nodded and then said, *"It has the symbol for enlightenment on it,"* pointing to the circular fissure on the left side of the rock that had a dot in the middle that was a slightly lighter color than the rest of the rock.

"That probably didn't start to show or become clear until after you had been carrying the rock for awhile," she said, adding, *"You are learning a lot."*

"Yes," I answered. *"I've been looking at that phrase from the Bodhisattva prayer: 'Mindfulness, born of inner silence,' and I am*

179

working on being silent and making choices that nurture rather than take me away from it. I've started to become aware that my body becomes tense just before the mind chatter starts. If I can relax in that moment, my mind remains quiet."

She smiled warmly at me, and nodded.

I continued, "*I have also been looking at what you said the other day about habitual energy. How if you have habitual energy in one area of your life, you have it everywhere, because it is all one. A lot of the time, I notice how I will say, 'Oh, it is just this one small area.' But now, I am seeing that it is not just that one area.*"

"*It will be so nice when you get past this karma. You are just scratching the surface,*" she said with feeling.

I nodded, knowing that developing a quiet mind was only a first step, and said, "*But, this is important.*"

"*Yes, it is, because of where it will lead you,*" she replied. Looking deeply at me a moment, she added, "*It is interesting how people's faces change. You must have noticed how your face has changed, gaining strength.*"

I nodded, smiling, gazing into the Wisdom Master's eyes as we stood in silence for a few moments.

Then she smiled gently and said, "*Well, have a good day.*"

"*You, too,*" I replied, beaming at her, then walked down the steps and headed on my way.

A few days later, I was in the kitchen going through the medicine cabinet. I had taken down the defibrillator to check the supplies. It was heavy and bulky and a little awkward to hold with just one hand. When I was almost done, I heard the bell ring for the afternoon meditation, so I quickly finished up what I was doing. As I was putting the defibrillator back up on the top shelf, I placed my right, rock-filled hand on the side of it, to try to lend some support and a little extra strength as I put it back up. It got caught on something; I could feel my left hand lose its grip. In that moment, I knew I was either going to drop the defibrillator or use my right hand to catch it and allow my rock to drop to the floor. I chose the latter. When my rock hit the floor, there was a loud cracking sound; I closed my eyes and grimaced, hoping the rock hadn't broken in half. Looking down in apprehension, I saw that a thin circular piece had been chipped off. It was the circular fissure that had formed the symbol of enlightenment. I looked around on the floor and found what was still intact of the chipped-off piece. I picked it up. My mind started to go wild. *What did this mean? What am I going to do? I broke my rock!* I managed to get a hold of myself before I completely freaked out. I took a few deep breaths. Then, shaking my head, said to myself, *"Oh, well, there is nothing I can do about it now, and I have to go or I will be late for the mediation."*

During meditation, I put the chip back in place, and held it there as if I thought I could join the pieces back together by sheer will. By this time, my rock had really become a friend, and I was a little upset that I had damaged it. I had liked the sign of enlightenment being on it. But then, I thought that I shouldn't be attached. Things change. My rock had been changing along with me. It had gotten increasingly smoother, and it was even changing color. It was no longer grey; it was becoming black. But then, I thought, *"It really isn't my rock; it is the Wisdom Master's. I broke the Wisdom Master's rock!"* As I continued to sit there, I remembered the Wisdom Master's saying that you can have anything you want as long as you aren't attached to it. I realized that I did want the rock repaired. If it couldn't be, that was okay, too, but I would prefer it. As I looked at my rock trying to figure out how it could be fixed, it occurred to me that maybe I could glue it. After meditation, I went downstairs to the shop and found some glue that was used for cement and ceramics. The directions said the pieces had to be held firmly for an hour and that it took 24 hours for it to dry completely. I spent the next hour holding the chip in place, willing it to stick. After an hour, it looked like it was going to work, but I was very careful with it for the next 24 hours. The rock looked just as it did before, except for a small piece at the top that had been completely shattered when it hit the floor. Now, my only concern was what the Wisdom Master was going to say when I told her.

The next day during the morning, I tired to find an opportunity to talk with the Wisdom Master but was unsuccessful. In the afternoon while I was in the kitchen, the Wisdom Master came in and sat down at a table. She talked with another apprentice for a minute and then said, *"Let me see your rock...if you can part with it for a few minutes."*

"I dropped it yesterday, and it broke," I said, walking towards her.

I offered her the rock, and she took it. It was the first time in weeks it had left my hand. I moved my fingers back and forth. It felt strange.

"Where?" she said. I pointed to the area. *"Oh, there is a fissure there,"* she said in a way that made me think it made sense for that part to chip off.

"I glued it back together," I said.

She laughed. *"We might make a stone mason out of you."* Then, looking intently at the rock, she said, "It is changing color."

I nodded. She looked at my hand again, noting a few small callouses that had formed. Then, she returned the rock to me, said goodbye to everyone, and headed home for the day.

After she left, I had to laugh at myself. It hadn't been a big deal at all. A phrase from one of the discourses popped into my mind, *"The reactive mind is like a fever."* Boy, was that true. I remembered what it felt like when I initially dropped my rock. The thoughts had been racing through my head like wildfire. It had taken me a second to quiet my mind and step back and get some perspective. But even after that, my mind kept wanting to worry and make up stories. It had taken perseverance not to let myself get all bent out of shape about it until I had a chance to talk with the Wisdom Master. It occurred to me then that this was part of what the Wisdom Master meant when she talked about being obsessive. The mind grabs hold of something, and it just keeps going in circles with it, usually downward spirals.

Over the next few weeks, I continued to carry my rock, delving deeper into the silence. During my walks in the forest, I would sometimes sit and listen to the pattern of the raindrops falling, and see the droplets of water hanging on the pine needles, making them look like they were decorated with tiny crystals. Many times, I saw deer grazing and birds flying. Once, when I was standing up on Amitabha hill looking out over the vista, a hawk flew up from the valley and circled around my head several times. It was close enough that I could see the different colors of its feathers. On one sunny day, I went for a walk out to the far creek. As I got closer, my eyes were caught by the sun reflecting off a spider web. There was a gentle breeze blowing, moving the web and causing the light to be reflected off of it like a many-faceted crystal. I just stood watching this for awhile, and when I looked up, I could see spider webs glistening everywhere. It made me think of 'dharma threads' holding the scene together.

I continued to uncover more of my habitual energy. I began to see how I had a pattern of not wanting to take the time to acknowledge someone as I passed by them. The incident with the Wisdom Master was not the first time I had done something like that. But with the Wisdom Master's assistance, I was becoming aware of the haughty arrogance I sometimes portrayed, and I started to see how it had been a source of many of the difficulties I had had in my life. I began to be very conscious of acknowledging others as I passed, bowing to their divinity, and laughing at myself when I felt the haughtiness rise up in me. But it seemed as soon as I discovered one habitual pattern and started working on it, another popped up. I decided that I just needed to keep moving forward, keep trusting, and stay vigilant in being mindful. If I got tripped up by my habitual energy, I just needed to see it for what it was, let it go without any mental chatter about it, and not pick it back up. I was no longer driven; I was allowing myself to be where I was, having the patience to allow the expansion to occur in me. By this point, I was carrying my rock in my dreams, too.

One afternoon, the Wisdom Master called me into her office. I came into the room and knelt down on the floor in front of her desk, sat back on my heels, and quietly waited to see what she would say. She had a folder full of papers in front of her. I realized it was the folder I had given her a few days before. It was full of stories by apprentices of their experiences with the Wisdom Master. When I had given her the folder, I had included a note explaining a few things and asking a couple of questions. At the end of the note, after much debate, I had included a postscript stating that I knew it was a lot of stories to go through, and was there anything else I could do to make that process easier.

The Wisdom Master looked at me, saying, *"I enjoy reading these stories. This is not laborsome. They make great bedtime stories."*

I smiled, glad she was enjoying them as much as I had and silently chuckling at myself for thinking it might be otherwise.

"How is your hand doing?" she asked.

I rose back up on my knees and showed her my hand, saying *"My wrist is a little sore."* It had started to bother me a bit; the muscles and tendons getting cramped and stiff from being held in the same position for so long. But I hadn't wanted to say anything. I was still learning so much from carrying the rock and didn't want to put it down yet.

"Are you wounded?" she asked.

"No," I said laughing, *"I'm not wounded."*

"You are still learning from it," she stated.

"Yes," I answered, but then added, *"I'll let you know if anything really starts to bother me."*

Later that day, as I was looking back over that conversation, I realized that writing that postscript at the end of my note to the Wisdom Master was my habitual way of operating when I perceived someone to be extremely busy and pressed for time. It was something I had learned as a child when interacting with my mother, who had a very demanding and time-consuming job. When I presented something to my mom, I always tried to make sure it was done in the most efficient way possible, and I only presented what absolutely had to have her attention. Otherwise, if it was too many things, like the huge stack of stories I had given the Wisdom Master, she would say she didn't have time to go through it all. I realized that the internal debate I had had over including the postscript or not, was a result of the pull between what I knew was correct, *not* including it, and my compulsive habitual behavior, which was *to* include it. When I saw that, I began to get a sense of the differences in the feelings between the two behaviors, so that next time, I would be able to catch myself.

As time went by, it began to get closer to the day when I had promised to pick up several other apprentices from the airport and bring them to Skycliffe for an empowerment. I hadn't driven since I received my rock. It hadn't seemed safe, and there was no real need for me to do so. Several other residents had offered to pick up things for me when they went out, so I hadn't lacked for anything. I knew I needed to talk to the Wisdom Master about it, but the moment hadn't seemed right yet.

Then one day, as I was walking back from helping to set up the shower tent in the campground, I ran into the Wisdom Master in the parking lot. She called me over, saying, *"Come over here a minute."*

I ran over and stood silently, concentrating on the presence of the Wisdom Master.

She looked penetratingly at my rock-filled hand for a few moments, as if she were making a decision. Then she said, *"Let me see your hand."*

185

I lifted the rock out of my hand and held my hand out to her. She studied it. Then, she said, *"Is the rock causing your hand to shake?"*

Surprised, I looked down at my hand. I hadn't noticed any shaking. I knew my fingers were cramped. I had been trying to stretch them out, which had been a little painful because they were so stiff. *"I hadn't noticed it shaking,"* I answered.

She considered my hand for a few moments more and then said, *"I am going to have you put the rock down now."*

"Okay," I replied.

"It has gotten to be a friend, so you can keep it," she added.

"Thank you," I said, slipping the rock into my pocket. I was happy that I could keep the rock; it had become my buddy over the past weeks, my partner in developing inner silence.

Later that day when I got back to my room, I took the rock out of my pocket and set it on my desk in front of a picture of the Wisdom Master. I sat there looking at both of them, feeling gratitude rise up and fill me. As I continued to sit there, it occurred to me that if I had not stumbled and lost the opportunity to go on that trip with the Wisdom Master, I would not have received my rock. I am sure I would have learned something valuable on the trip, but I knew with certainty that I would not trade the experiences I had had over the past several weeks for anything. I was starting to learn about true openness, and I knew the adventure was just beginning.

Stupa Flowers

In the Stupa Garden
The Wisdom Master knelt beside me,
Hands full of dark,
Rich earth.
She helped me by patting it
Firmly
Between new plants,
Her hands gently caressing
The tiny purple blossoms.

"Put some   here   and   here   and   here,"
She said

As She moved
Around me,
Like a Whisper,
Through me,
Inside me.

And I,
Dreaming
In the Silence of Her voice
Entered The

BETWEEN...
Consumed

187

In the
Oneness of
Hand and Earth,
Of
Earth and Flower
Of
Wisdom Master and Apprentice.

In the
Oneness of
Hand and Earth,
Of
Earth and Flower
Of
Wisdom Master and Apprentice.

I Am Worthy

After sharing with Wisdom Master Maticintin about the long-term relationship I had with a person who would not make a marriage commitment, I was told, *"You are worthy; a divine being."* Looking at that statement, I realized I was not being true to myself by having a relationship that I did not want and was able to end the relationship.

Nothing Happens by Accident

One day during a Teaching out by the Stupa, Wisdom Master Maticintin incorporated some aspects of relativity, quantum physics, and mathematics into her talk. This piqued my interest to do some further reading, so on my next day off, my husband, who is also an apprentice, and I went browsing through the science section of a large, local bookstore.

As I was sitting on the floor looking over some books, I felt a strong tingling sensation on my crown chakra and thought, *"It feels like the Wisdom Master is looking this way,"* but I didnt say anything about it at the time. Eventually, we purchased a few books and went on our way.

The next day, back at Skycliffe, we were again gathered out by the Stupa for a Teaching when the Wisdom Master said, *"I looked right at you yesterday at the bookstore as you were sitting on the floor looking at some books."* Then, turning to my husband, she said, *"You looked directly at me without seeing me, even though I stood within a few feet of you."* She added, *"I wanted some space to myself that day so I chose not to be visible to you."* Needless to say, we were both taken aback.

On another occasion several weeks later, I was in the Wal-Mart restroom in Kelowna. I was deeply self-absorbed at the time. There were some other women in the restroom that I was oblivious to, so I was not focused on them or on my surroundings. As I intently washed my hands, a woman stepped up close to me, placing her head very near mine. I glanced up and nearly jumped out of my skin when I saw my Wisdom Master's grinning face, and I laughed self-consciously at having been caught so completely unaware. I was rather chagrined, and quickly left the 'scene of the crime,' though I thought about the encounter for some time afterwards.

As we discussed the Wal-Mart incident the next day, the Wisdom Master commented, *"Nothing happens by accident. Do you recall our prior encounter at the bookstore?"* She said, *"In both cases, you were so strongly focused on me that it caused our paths to cross."*

A Sleep-Time Dream

I learned a good lesson about fear in a sleep-time dream. In it, Wisdom Master Maticintin was talking to some apprentices, including me, about garbage and started to pull everything out of my garbage can piece by piece. I was horrified, because I had something in it that I did not want her to find. Each time she took something out, I cringed. But then, nothing of importance came out, and it so happened that what I was afraid that she might find turned out to be an empty cottage cheese container! I was relieved; it was nothing at all. I realized that what I fear is really of no significance, especially once it is exposed and brought into the light.

Letting Go

I had brought my nineteen-year-old male cat with me for a long-term stay at Skycliffe. We settled in, and he loved it here. It was his first experience of being able to be an "outdoor cat," because previously, my fears for his safety would not allow him to be outside.

Wisdom Master Maticintin had hinted that I should let him explore outside some. I had resisted, and then she would kid around by saying little things like, "*I think you are right; the traffic is just awful out here.*" (We lived in a large fenced-in area that was closed in with gates at several entrances.) Or, she might say something like, "*You are so wise to keep him away from the vicious animals here on the property.*" (There were none.) So it went, until I had to laugh at myself and ask him, "*Well, old boy, are you ready for this?*"

And he wasn't; it took him a week to get beyond the front porch. He began his explorations slowly but had become a happy independent explorer with a definite mind of his own. It was a joy to watch his transitions and accomplishments, and it triggered me to branch out of my own limitations as well.

The Hood

One morning as I left the kitchen to attend meditation, I threw a purple, hooded jacket over my robe. It was cool outside. I walked up the steps to the Temple, removed my shoes, and entered. To my surprise, the Wisdom Master was standing just inside the door, and she smiled at me as I entered. *"Nice socks,"* she commented, looking down at the fuzzy, purple socks on my feet. *"Thanks,"* I replied. Then, she looked at me and asked if I was going to wear my 'savant's hood' into the Temple. Gasping and blushing bright pink, since I was not a savant, I realized that she was referring to the purple, hooded jacket that I had forgotten to remove before going in. The Wisdom Master laughed, and I joined her in laughter, as I exited to remove my jacket.

Before the Teaching that day, I remember that the Wisdom Master looked my way and commented that she used to like to wear a superman cape when she was a child. I smiled and blushed again. We all laughed, and she said something to the effect that blushing raises one's energy and is an expression of naturalness. As I sat listening on my cushion, I felt my heart swell in love. I realized that relaxing and learning to JUST BE allows me to do what I want most: to open myself to my Wisdom Master.

Slug

I was trekking toward the horse shed when I heard Wisdom Master Maticintin's voice, *"Oh, look at this! It's such a different color."*

I walked towards the Wisdom Master, assuming she was talking to me. Well, it was a large yellow slug she was looking at. I said, *"Oh, its a yellow slug."* (The only color slugs I had seen on the island up to this point were black.)

End of story? Hardly…the Wisdom Master said, *"The slug is in the middle of the walkway and might be injured if it remains here."* I was thinking to myself, *'Whoops, I should have kept walking to the horse shed,'* because I had a hunch what was coming up.

Her next words were, *"Would you please pick up the slug and place it in a safe place so it will not be stepped on?"*

I was right in tune with her words, yet at the same time, I was thinking, *'Yes, this is good that she brings it to my attention about the environment and the interconnectedness of all things.'* Well, gee, as soon as this thought came up, it was followed by, *'Yo, she wants me to pick up this THING!'* Funny, how the mind can switch from being in tune with the oneness of all life…. to the slug now becoming a 'THING' in my mind.

I said, *"Me?"* and the Wisdom Master said, *"Yes, you. Do you see anyone else here?"* I replied, *"You've got to be kidding."* Well, let me say, the conversation continued. It became a dialogue of playful dance, with my trying to evade the issue. I caught myself in the dance (a box) and eventually snapped back to the moment. For me, the transition was in realizing that it is okay to be one with the spontaneous dance of life, knowing the dance is just the dance; it is the illusion. The dance becomes merely a tool.

195

With the Wisdom Master, there is always Teaching. Indeed, there was more than a playful exchange of words going on. I BLEW IT! The more she talked, the harder it was for me to pick up the slug. Maybe the most important part of this story was the moment I saw that while I was being made aware of my disregard of the feelings of the slug, the slug curled up before my eyes, literally shrank. The Wisdom Master continued to speak to me of 'sentient beings' consisting of *all* living creatures. I cannot put into words the difficulty I experienced hearing her words and seeing the slug that I could not touch curl up even more. Her words continued to hammer in my head. In the silence between her words, I stepped out of myself. It was like I was in tune with the feeling of the slug and felt the slug did not want me to touch it. It didnt want me to touch it because of my ATTITUDE. This caused a further resistance.

I had never experienced this before. I do not cry.... but oh, how I was crying inside. Here, I not only affected this slug's feeling with my warped attitude, but this caused it to curl up.

At that moment, the Wisdom Master picked up the slug and moved it to a safe place on the grass. End of conversation. She left, crossing in front of my body with no words and an expression on her face I cannot put in writing.... a look that will stick in my mind for a long time.

She walked to her house. I dropped the horse feed carrier in front of me and went to my room. Minutes later, I received a call from the Wisdom Master to meet her at her house. I quickly showed up feeling sick to my stomach. I was thinking, *'Here I am a resident apprentice, and I can't even follow a simple instruction. I not only failed the Wisdom Master, I FAILED!*

The rest of the story becomes easy to write because after sitting with the Wisdom Master in her silence (a long silence, I will add), she spoke of sentient beings and how we affect all life. I was crying inside without tears, but crying. Her words brought clarity of thought.

It seemed like minutes later she said, *"I wonder how the slug is doing? Would you like to walk out with me to see if it is okay?"*

I joined her to see that the slug was no longer curled up, but very elongated with two tentacle-type things sticking out. I spontaneously said, *"I want to pick up the slug."* She said, *"You don't have to do that, you know."*

Well, I not only picked up the slug with my bare hand, but I had it resting in the palm of my hand. There was nothing in my mind. I only felt this slug now comfortable and relaxed in my hand.

Nothing To Talk About

I had asked to talk with the Wisdom Master to get clarity about something she had said to me a couple of months prior. Of course, I had in mind to discuss what I had seen during those months regarding what I thought she meant and to hear what she actually did mean. In the course of beginning to explain to her, I said that when I try to focus, I start talking in my mind about focusing. She said, *"There is nothing to talk about."* In that moment, I got it. Even though I was aware of the self that wanted to discuss what I came to talk about, I gave it no attention. I didn't argue with it or resist it; my mind was quiet. My attention was on the Wisdom Master and the mental silence. I just started laughing. She said, *"It is good to laugh at it,"* and then she repeated, *"There is nothing to talk about."* I was still laughing, and I said, *"Your answer is always the same, and it is right on."* I left with no mental chatter and a feeling of freedom.

Yawn

One day as I left the kitchen, I was unaware that I was 'mull-ing,' staring at myself and my PROBLEMS. The Wisdom Master walked past me and headed up to the Temple. She looked at me and patted her hand to her wide open mouth in an *'it's so boring'* gesture. I was shocked that she considered my really big PROBLEMS boring. Then, it slowly dawned on me that she was giving me an important lesson. She had alerted me to the fact that I had been self-absorbed, and I realized that my PROBLEMS had actually seemed pretty *interesting* to me; I must be really *attached* to them. I needed to be as bored as the Wisdom Master. As I learned to become more and more mindful, I began to observe myself in my 'worry mode' and to bring back the image of the Wisdom Master walking away, yawning at me. Her big yawn just had to make me laugh and was a great help as I began to learn to shift my attention... away from myself.

Negative Attitudes

We had been using a small, local post office to send our mailings and to pick up our mail. The postmaster was a sour individual, nearing retirement, and very negative in his attitude. He was full of complaints and criticisms. After one particular situation, the Wisdom Master decided that we would no longer deal there; we would go to a larger post office some distance away, where the environment was more cordial.

Then, one day, our former postmaster was complaining to one of the students that the postal service was threatening to close down the small post office for lack of business. When the Wisdom Master heard this, I remember her turning to me and saying, *"Please tell him that if he is happy to have our business, then we are happy to bring our business back."*

When I relayed this message, the postmaster looked at me for a long moment and then said, *"I would be happy to have your business."* He tried very hard to have a positive attitude towards us for the rest of the time until he retired.

"That's Shanunpa"

One day, I happened to be in the Wisdom Master's house doing something and decided I would shake out the rugs which had gotten littered by many feet, animal and human, coming and going.

Inside the Wisdom Masters house, there were many throw rugs placed in a particular way so as to catch most of the dirt the animals (two dogs and a cat) brought in; but at that moment, I hadn't made the connection that they were there primarily for the animals. I began to take them outdoors, two at a time, to shake out. I knew enough about myself to realize that taking more than two would put me in danger of not returning the rugs to their assigned spots; however, in spite of that, I decided to take the last three rugs out together. Naturally, the Wisdom Master entered the house at that moment.

"What are you doing?" she asked.

"Shaking out the rugs," I replied, observing her hopefully to see if she might leave so I could try and figure out what went where.

"Why, thank you," she said, and stood watching. I felt the stirrings of anxiety as I realized she would know immediately that I couldn't remember precisely where the rugs should go. I proceeded to lay them in the general vicinity of where they had been.

"Wait a moment," she said. *"The animals don't walk toward the wood stove to get to the kitchen."*

"They don't?" I asked, thinking if it were me, I would head to the stove first to warm up.

"No, they don't," she said. *"You have to think like they think. Get down on all fours and be in Shanunpa with them."* (Shanunpa is a Native American word that means to imitate something until you merge consciousness with it, to know it).

I got down on the floor and began walking like a dog and then a cat, replacing the rugs as I moved. I stood and surveyed my work, nodding in satisfaction.

"They aren't going to take the long way," the Wisdom Master commented, and I looked again, noting that I had made a route that was sort of L-shaped.

"Oh, I see," I replied, now seeing the picture. I had still been 'thinking like a person,' placing the rugs as I might have walked through the house, not as a dog or cat hungry for their evening meal, heading in a direct route from the front door to the kitchen.

Quickly I moved the rugs into a direct line from one point to the other.

"Now, that's shanunpa," she said, *"To think like something else thinks, you must become one with them."*

Sugar

I stood with the Wisdom Master at the sink in the kitchen. *"If I were you, I would go off sugar,"* she said. She had been working with me for some time on a serious health issue, and so I nodded in agreement. She told me that included any type of sugar, including honey and maple syrup. Again, I agreed in appreciation of her advice. I stopped eating desserts or anything with any type of sugar.

I was doing well for about three months. Then, one day, I decided that one cookie could not hurt. After a few days I had some dessert at lunch. It is interesting now to remember how I convinced myself that surely the Wisdom Master did not mean that I was not to have sugar ALL THE TIME. I reasoned that staying off sugar for that length of time had not really helped much. So, pretty soon, I was eating dessert again just about every day.

Then, after a short time, the Wisdom Master called me into her office. I remember she said that it looked like I had 'given up' by going back on sugar. If that was the case, she said that she *"could no longer work with me."* I looked into her eyes and my heart sank. I felt as though the room was dissolving in darkness, and I was dissolving along with it. *"I'm sorry,"* was all I could manage, as words began to fail me. She was right. I had not been honest with her or myself, and I had 'given up' in a way I had not even admitted to myself. I felt 'surrounded'...by the truth; in that truth, I had an unexpected sense of illumination or light-ness as the Wisdom Master put the situation straight out for me to see. In taking responsibility for my actions, I could now reaffirm my commitment, renewing my resolve to do all I could for the health of my body. I also learned not to interpret what the Wisdom Master asks me to do, to take her advice to the letter. She acts only out of love.

Walking in Circles

My husband and I rented a home to be closer to the Wisdom Master. The home we rented was ideal in every way for our needs and was in walking distance from our Wisdom Master, making it possible to visit her daily and get some physical exercise as well.

The first thing I noticed about the morning walk was that it required an upward spiral on a hill that looked to me as though it went on forever. By the time I reached the top where the road leveled out, I was puffing and winded. I came to dread that first part of the walk. After several days of making the jaunt, I noticed a pattern to my behavior. I would leave the house in good spirits, start up the hill with my eyes focused ahead, and begin to say to myself, '*I don't know if I can make it. It's too steep and too long.*' Soon my steps slowed and I was barely moving. Eventually, of course, I reached the top, but not without a great effort.

One day, I decided I had heard enough of my own complaining. It was time to do something different. I began focusing my attention around me, often watching my feet as they moved forward. Pretty soon, I was at the top of the hill, still puffing a bit, but not at all tired, and certainly not bored from listening to myself complain.

The next awakening in this story occurred for me through an experience with the Wisdom Master upon leaving the Temple one evening after mediation. As several of us walked toward the parking lot, the Wisdom Master paused and waited for me to catch up, extending her arm for me to loop mine through. We walked for a bit before arriving at her car where there is also a large pile of wood chips. We began walking, arm in arm, around the pile of chips and the Wisdom Master asked me, *"What are we doing?"'*

"*We're walking in circles, Wisdom Master Maticintin,*" I replied.

"*Yes, we are,*" she agreed, pausing a moment. "*If you realize that, there is nothing else to learn.*"

I stopped walking and looked at her, knowing she was Teaching me something important but not sure it was penetrating.

Seeing my confusion, she repeated, "*If you realize that, there is nothing else to learn.*" Then she turned and walked away.

The next morning, I found myself again looking toward 'the top of the hill.' Much to my surprise and delight, what I now saw was a road that wound upward toward the top of the hill. *It didn't look far, and it didn't look steep.* It was just the road that I was walking on. As I walked forward on it, I was able to enjoy the scenery around me and appreciate the way the road disappeared into in the sky. In no time at all, I was at the top.

As I shared the 'hill' story with the Wisdom Master that morning, she said, "*Do you remember what we were doing last night after we left the Happy House?*"

"*Yes,*" I replied as the light went on. "*We were walking in circles, just as I have been doing by repeating the same habitual thoughts and behavior patterns all my life.*"

"*Now you understand your experience with the hill this morning,*" she said.

No Fear

"You *are going to leave Skycliffe, get a job, and support your-self without any of your mother's money, for at least a year,"* Wisdom Master Maticintin said, looking directly at me as I sat across from her on the purple cushion in her office.

My eyes grew wide, and a knot formed in my throat. I tried to swallow, but my mouth had gone dry. I said nothing.

She continued, *"Recently, I have been looking at all the things I did before I took my seat here. They all helped to prepare me. You are naïve. You need to go and have some experience, so that when you come back, you can spiritually soar. This is part of your training, and I will be your buddy through it."*

My insides were in turmoil. I finally managed to swallow, but that did nothing to ease the tightness in my throat. I bit my lower lip and kept my eyes fastened on the Wisdom Master, still unable to speak, her words echoing my inner fears.

"I don't care what kind of job you get; you could sweep floors," she said, waving her hands in an unspoken 'whatever works.' Then, she continued, *"You don't think you can live in the world without compromising yourself, but you can. I have always been true to my-self."*

Leaning forward, she said, *"I think you will find the world isn't what you think it is."* She paused, looking at me as I raised my eyebrows, and then tilted her head to the side, saying, *"Or maybe it is."*

"You are almost thirty," she stated, as I shifted in my seat and looked down at my hands. *"At thirty, you will be set in your ways, an old dog. Now is the time to break these patterns. Do you see what I am saying?"*

With my chin tucked into my chest, and my head tilted to the side, I looked up with a combination of a grimace and an embarrassed smile on my face, and nodded, *"Yeah..."*

"We talked about this," she said.

I nodded again, lowering my eyes, remembering the conversation in her car the previous week.

Sitting in the passenger seat of the Wisdom Master's car, I had turned and asked, *"How do you know if a feeling is you or someone else? I feel like the surface waters are being disturbed, but underneath, there is calm."*

She had gazed at me, and said, *"If the surface is disturbed, it usually means there is a big disturbance underneath the water. But the wind can sometimes blow across the water and make ripples."*

"That is what I mean, then. The wind disturbing the surface," I had replied.

"You have to become quiet inside and then ask, 'Is there anything wrong?' If the answer is, no, then it's not you," she had answered.

I had tried to quiet my mind, but I couldn't stop the mind chatter.

"So what is it?" she had asked.

I had tried again. The uneasy, restless feeling had still been there. I couldn't articulate it. I didn't want it to be there. I had opened my mouth, but nothing had come out. My fear was choking me.

"You can't stuff things," she had said.

In a rush, I had said, *"I want to know that I can take care of myself completely, independent of my mom."* Even though technically I was doing that with a sum of money my mom had given me (no strings attached), a part of me couldn't let go of the fact that she had given it to me, and I hadn't earned it myself. It had been bothering me for a couple of months. Along with it were many other doubts about my readiness, which I had picked up from my family and friends, as well as desires to do things in the world, which had been stirred up by movies and books, creating all sorts of confusion in me.

"If there is something you feel you need to do, you can go and do it. No one is tied here, and the door will always be open to you. You are still in the first stage of growing up. You haven't even fallen madly in love yet," she had said kindly to me.

"I know everything comes from inside me..." I had said, but then hesitated, trying to see through the confusion I had created.

"I think this comes from outside you, not inside; facsimiles that have attached themselves to you. And you are curious," she had replied, smiling, a twinkle in her eye, *"That is what I think."*

I was brought back to the present by the sound of the Wisdom Master's voice. *"Now, I want you to be safe. I think you have enough good karma and inner wisdom that you will be fine. And after a year, if you want to come back, you can. Maybe not the same room, but there will be a place for you. If there isn't space, we will make room,"* she said firmly, easing my fears.

"I would like you to stay for the Lankavatara Sutra (a class that was taking place in a few months)." She paused, looking at me, *"If you want to?"*

"Oh, I do," I said, nodding my head vigorously.

"Now, I don't want you to talk to your mother or anyone else about this for awhile. Just sit with it and come to your own decisions. You can take your time. I am not in any rush to get rid of you. You can take two, three,...six months, if you want. And whenever it starts to be too much, feel free to pop in here and talk to me."

"Okay." I said, biting the left side of my lower lip and taking a deep breath.

She smiled lovingly at me. I got up and bowed, saying, *"Thank you,"* and left the office.

Later, back down in the dining room, my feelings were in turmoil. I was trying to remain positive, and a part of me was excited about having an adventure, a mission, but another part was deeply saddened that I had to leave Skycliffe to have it. During the afternoon chanting of the *Wish-Fulfilling Gem Mantra*, it finally hit me. I bit my lip, holding back the tears that threatened to fall. I knew if they started, I wouldn't be able to stop them. I went through the rest of the day trying to keep myself busy, so that I couldn't think about what had happened. That night, as I lay in bed, I finally let the tears come. I only slept a few hours, mostly tossing and turning.

The next morning, I got into my car and drove away from Skycliffe. As I drove down the road, I felt the urge to go faster and faster, to lose myself in the speed. But then the thought of deer crossing the road eased my foot from the gas. I went over to the new coffee shop in Midway and got on the internet. I researched rent rates and possible jobs in different cities. My mind ran rampant, caught in one emotion and then another.

I finally got up and departed, not wanting to think about leaving anymore. Back at Skycliffe, I got lost in watching movies, but the situation continued to hang over me, and I had another restless night. Thursday morning, I finally decided that I was not going to think about leaving anymore. I was just going to keep my attention on being here, on what I wanted, and then maybe when my six months were up, I wouldn't have to leave.

That day, Wisdom Master Maticintin gave a Teaching: *"You manifest your life from your mental imagery. I just reflect back to you what you put out."* She turned and looked directly at me, her eyes widening as she said, *"If someone is uncertain about staying, they can leave."* She turned away, continuing to speak, *"If someone is living in the present moment, and learning from the experiences that arise from that, I usually leave them alone because they are learning."* I glanced down at my hands, realizing how little I had been living in the present moment. *"You can change any situation you do not want,"* and turning back towards me, she said emphatically, *"and you can change it instantly, by changing your mental imagery."* I quickly looked up at the Wisdom Master, her words igniting hope and illuminating a way out of my situation.

That night and the next day, I looked deeply at what had happened, and I began to see how the meeting in the Wisdom Master's office was just a reflection of the mental imagery and fear I was carrying inside of me. The Wisdom Master gave me what I feared the most because that was where I was putting all my attention. It was this fear that I carried that allowed all these outside facsimiles, mind sets I learned from others, which I did not want, to attach to me and make me believe I had to live them out. Then it hit me: I don't have to live out this fear. I can change my mental imagery any time I want, if I can get to a place where I see the fear is an illusion and let it go.

I let out a deep sigh, because I could still feel the fear inside of me, and I was not sure I could let it go. I turned my attention away from that thought and started to study intensely every discourse I had that might help me. I read the Teachings every free moment I had, writing down phrases that resonated with me; and as I read and wrote, I perceived more of how the situation evolved from my mental imagery and the placement of my attention.

Friday evening, sitting at a table in the empty dining room, I reread a quote from the Wisdom Master: *"To trust means that we are certain of someone or something that we want in our life. We simply know, and we put fear of success (or failure) aside, and give ourselves to what we want. Giving ourselves to what we want is an impeccable way of living wholeheartedly."* In that moment, I saw that the key to letting go of my fear was trust. There was a shift in me, as I chose to trust, and I became filled with a sense of well-being and inner calm, which I hadn't felt in weeks. Energy surged through my body, and I felt expansive and free, in control of my life. I WAS the dreamer. I laughed. I laughed at the situation I had created, and I laughed from the joy of knowing I could change it

That night I stayed up until the early morning writing a letter to the Wisdom Master about my realizations. I put it in her box before the morning meditation, and when I came into the Temple for the 11am Teaching, the letter was on my cushion. I opened it up and across the top I read: *"Did you have a good laugh at how one's mind works? Did you laugh at yourself?"* I grinned, joy surging through me. A fleeting thought of *'Does this mean I can stay?'* passed through my mind, but I didn't attach to it. I focused on living the present moment.

Later, after the Mantra meditation, the Wisdom Master called down and asked for me to come up to her house by taking the trail through the woods. I had never walked to her house before, so I got directions. Then, I grabbed a walking stick and set out; my whole body tingling with anticipation. When I got there, the clearing around her house was full of deer, but they ran away into the trees as I entered. I paused a moment, and then continued quietly making my way around the house. As I got closer, I saw the Wisdom Master peering around the corner; she said, *"Hurry up and get inside so the deer can come back."* I quickly crossd the remaining distance, took off my shoes, and stepped inside. I hesitated in the entrance; not sure what to do next. Walking across the room, the Wisdom Master smiled warmly at me. *"Take off your jacket and come sit down,"* she said, indicating the couch in front of the large windows that look out onto the area where she feeds the deer.

I sat down, and the Wisdom Master joined me. We waited and watched as the deer cautiously ventured back, eager to eat. Finally, she turned to me and asked, *"So, what was the bottom-line of your letter?"*

Without any thought, I replied, *"I want to stay."*

She beamed at me, saying, *"Okay. We can do that."* My face broke into a huge smile. *"It is always your choice,"* she said.

211

"I know," I softly replied.

"Before, you were kind of...," she paused, searching for the correct word, *"flaky. I couldn't touch you."* I nodded, seeing the truth in her words.

We went back to watching the deer, and the Wisdom Master pointed out different things to me about them. Finally, I asked, *"Do any birds come and eat after the deer?"* She replied, *"Oh, lots of birds come. Usually, the magpies first; they are the scouts."* Eventually, one magpie did come, and we watched him while he ate the leftover corn off the ground. The Wisdom Master said, *"There are some advantages to being the scout,"* referring to the fact that the magpie got to eat, while the other birds waited in the trees. Then she said, *"It pays to not have fear."*

"Yes, it does." I answered with conviction, thinking not only of the magpie, but also of myself.

www.HUMUH.org

√ Check Here

☐ I would like to receive information about other books by Wisdom Master Maticintin.
☐ I would like to receive information about becoming a student of HÜMÜH.
☐ I would like to be added to your mailing list and receive information about events with Wisdom Master Maticintin.
☐ I would like to receive *free* the Daily Wisdom Teaching by e-mail.

Please Print Clearly or Call: 1(800) 336-6015

Name: _____

Address: _____

City & State/Province: _____

Zip/Postal Code: _____ Country: _____

E-Mail: _____

√ Check Here

☐ I would like to receive information about other books by Wisdom Master Maticintin.
☐ I would like to receive information about about becoming a student of HÜMÜH.
☐ I would like to be added to your mailing list and receive information about events with Wisdom Master Maticintin.
☐ I would like to receive *free* the Daily Wisdom Teaching by e-mail.

Please Print Clearly or Call: 1(800) 336-6015

Name: _____

Address: _____

City & State/Province: _____

Zip/Postal Code: _____ Country: _____

E-Mail: _____

HÜMÜH™
Transcendental Awareness Institute
The Jeweled Path of Transcendental Wisdom™
P.O. Box 2700
Oroville, WA 98844
USA

HÜMÜH™
Transcendental Awareness Institute
The Jeweled Path of Transcendental Wisdom™
P.O. Box 701
Osoyoos, BC V0H 1V0
Canada